Collective
Coaching Wisdom

for Youth
Baseball

David A. Ham

Janice B. Sibley

D1456360

CRM | CRM Publishers ▪ Derwood, Maryland

Collective Coaching Wisdom for Youth Baseball
by David A. Ham and Janice B. Sibley

ISBN 0-9746920-0-X

Printed in the United States of America

Throughout the book, the tradenames of some organizations and products have been used, and no such uses are intended to convey endorsements or other affiliations with the book. Little League is a registered trademark of Little League Baseball Incorporated. Babe Ruth League is a registered trademark of Babe Ruth League, Inc. Clark C. Griffith Collegiate Baseball League is a registered trademark of Clark Griffith Baseball League. Wiffle is a registered trademark of The Whiffle Ball, Incorporated. Foxtail is a registered trademark of Klutz Company. Frisbee is a registered trademark of Mattel, Inc.

Cover Design: Franz & Company, Inc.
Editing Assistance: William A. McNamara, Jr.

Published by:
CRM Publishers
P.O. Box 5706 Derwood, Maryland 20855-0706
301-527-1667 ph 800-527-6991 (toll free) 301-527-0771 fax
http://www.crmpublishers.com

Publisher's Cataloging-in-Publication
(Provided by Quality Books, Inc.)

Ham, David A.
    Collective coaching wisdom for youth baseball / David
A. Ham, Janice B. Sibley.
    p. cm.
    Includes index.
    "A 'hometown heroes' book."
    ISBN 0-9746920-0-X

    1. Baseball for children--Coaching.   I. Sibley,
Janice B. II. Title.

GV880.4.H36 2004   796.357'62
                 QBI03-200892

For young baseball players, their coaches, and all those who cheer enthusiastically from the bleachers …

… in the Ham, Sibley, and Bain families … and everywhere.

Contents

SECTION 3 — Coaches' Memorable Stories 179

Foreword

At the heart of this book are the "word-of-mouth" thoughts and ideas from a few of youth baseball's coaching hometown heroes. Chances are you could find such a hero within your own community – a neighbor or friend who does an extraordinary job of coaching youth teams, who knows how to teach baseball fundamentals in a fun and encouraging way, having mastered the challenging art of coaching kids. There are lots of coaching heroes like this out there – we simply captured the wisdom of a few of the best to share with you.

How did we find these coaching heroes? Our search for extraordinary coaches led us to contacts with youth baseball leagues all across America, from Maine to Alaska, looking for hometown heroes with the right stuff who were willing to share their coaching tips and ideas, and tell us how they developed their unique and positive coaching styles. For the most part, the coaches we've highlighted in this book were recommended to us by their leagues because they hold the sport of youth baseball in its proper perspective – that winning is so much more than runs on a scoreboard.

Sure, as you read through the hometown hero biographies scattered throughout this book, you'll notice that many of these coaches have led teams to various levels of league, regional, state, or national championships. But, there are also many who have never captured a championship title. Just the same, we believe that extraordinary coaches exist at all levels. These hometown heroes understand that encouraging kids to learn, exhibiting positive sportsmanship, and making it fun are factors that far outweigh wins and losses.

Many of the suggestions in this book are clearly designed to favor sportsmanship, fun, encouragement, and fairness. You may not agree with all the ideas we've offered – some might not work well for your particular team or fit your coaching philosophy – but we have intentionally included as many different thoughts as possible, even conflicting ideas when appropriate, so that you can pick and choose your favorites as you develop your own unique coaching style.

By design, we specifically did not create this book as an extensive reference on youth baseball rules or explain every fundamental technique for teaching kids the sport. For those basics, you can walk into almost any bookstore or browse the collections of online book dealers and you will find lots of excellent books on teaching baseball fundamentals such as hitting, pitching, catching, fielding, and base running.

Instead, this book offers dozens of ideas on organizing your team, conducting fun but effective practices, coaching with encouragement and good sportsmanship during games, and dozens of other "not in the rulebook" tips for coaching youth baseball like a hometown hero!

David Ham and Janice Sibley

About the Authors

Picture a white-fenced backyard in the northeast corner of Maryland with the greenest grass you've ever seen, a few patches of white clover heads, and a few honey bees flying from one clover to another. A skinny 9-year old boy with jet black hair lives there with his sister and two brothers.

He spends his summer days barefoot and shirtless, sweating in the summer sun as he throws a well-worn, grass-stained baseball from one end of the yard to the other. He's not throwing the ball to a person. He's just throwing it … then walking to the other end of the yard and picking it up … then throwing it again. He's been doing this for hours. The smile on his face gives away that he's the most content kid on earth.

As he throws, he remembers the countless times he and his dad have played catch in that yard. He also thinks about how, on game days, he helps his dad load the lawn tractor into the back of the family jeep, then head out to the ball park to drag the dirt infield and get rid of all the rocks. The little boy unknowingly learns about dedication and volunteerism.

The little boy continues to play baseball in Little League, in high school, and in college. Then he practices dedication and volunteerism by coaching his own son's youth baseball teams.

• • • • •

Picture a skinny little girl with a long blondish ponytail sitting on the grassy sidelines of a school yard baseball diamond, watching her brother's team play a game under the bright afternoon southern California sun. Her dad is coaching her brother's team of 8- and 9-year olds in a Little League game. She watches her dad encourage every young player who steps up to the plate, "Come on Tommy. You can do it. Just watch the ball all the way in." Then, her dad calls out to the other boys to cheer their teammate on. The little girl unknowingly learns about positive coaching and team spirit.

The little girl's mom is sitting on the grass beside her and her sister. Earlier that afternoon the girl had helped her mom haul the big bag of baseball equipment up to the field. Her mom often did that to help out her dad so he could work a few minutes longer at the office before heading to the field himself. The little girl unknowingly learns about commitment and teamwork.

The little girl never plays baseball in Little League, or high school, or college, but grows up to sit on the grassy sidelines of countless other baseball fields while cheering for her own two sons as they step up to the plate.

• • • • •

The grown up boy and girl become coach and parent on the same baseball team, compare notes on exemplary coaching … then decide to find some of those coaches and write a book about them. Both David Ham and Janice Sibley now live in suburban Maryland with their respective families and their minivans forever filled with bats, bags, hats, gloves, and post-game snacks for youth baseball teams.

Our Thanks

We owe thanks to many people for their time, effort, and support during the writing of this book.

There are friends and colleagues who served as concept and copy reviewers during various stages of book development: Lisa Lahti, Shannon McBay, Kevin Mulroe, Bill Borchardt, Dan, Nancy, and Chase Brackley, John Cermak, Brennon Ham, Will McNamara, David Glick, Kim Siegert, Warren Winker, and Eileen Wong.

There are youth baseball league commissioners and presidents from all over the country who readily and enthusiastically assisted us by nominating and locating the hometown hero coaches we interviewed for this book: David Adams, Jay Bennett, Laura Black, Mary Ciacci, Bob DeChiaro, Bob Denherder, Becky Evans, Breck Parker, Barry Phillips, Phil Quartet, Ruth Sterling, Diane Wagner, and Hal Yamaguchi.

There are mentors and family members who, throughout our own youth and adulthood, have molded our viewpoints on dedication, fair play, winning with grace, losing with dignity, and always trying our best: Joe and Julie Bain, Earl and Iva Ham, Mike Bales, Crisi Ham, Rick, Patrick, and Sean Anderson, Dave and Robin Sibley, Jo McGlin, Jim Bain, Steve and Chuck Ham, Anthony Bering, Bob Shallcross, Charles Kasinec, Neil Taylor, Jr., Ward Welch, Ken Dollenger, Kent and Wayne Fuesel, Lora Nedimyer, Steve Ames, Steven Paul, Michael Cutlip, Clyde Brammer, Smoke Eldreth, Bill Gambill, Bob Barnett, Jim Gibney, Manley Pierce, Stan Barnes, and Joe Click.

All of these individuals played a role in the conceptualization and development of this book, and we thank them for their efforts.

In addition, we wish to acknowledge the professional expertise of our editing assistant, William A. McNamara, Jr., who proofread our copy and saved us from a rash of embarrassing phone calls and emails from English grammar teachers around the country. We also wish to acknowledge the creative talents of Franz & Company, Inc. for providing us with an incredible cover design that perfectly visualizes the theme of the book. Finally, we want to thank Derek Hacopian Baseball Academy for lending us their pitching tarp during our photo shoot and Patrick Cermak, Brennon Ham, Mike Sibley, and Chris Sibley for posing like "pros" for many of the book's photographs.

A Brief Introduction —
How to Use This Book

☐ *This coaching book is different!*

This book is not just another coaching fundamentals book. Rather, it offers you a wealth of practical coaching tips, drills, and advice — "word of mouth" ideas all passed on from extraordinary youth baseball coaches in their hometowns all across America — for organizing your team, running productive practices, inspiring teamwork and sportsmanship during games, and making baseball fun for kids.

No matter what page you open to, you will get something out of this book. If you're a novice coach, you will find lots of drills and coaching advice to keep in your back pocket for whenever you need them. If you're a seasoned coaching veteran, you'll pick up new ideas to liven up your established coaching routines. These are real tips from everyday people who have learned how to be extraordinary youth baseball coaches — the ones that all kids look up to and remember fondly as they grow up.

☐ *Find information quickly ... no lengthy reading required.*

All the information in this book is organized for quick reading, one paragraph or a few pages at a time.

- Section 1: Our coaches' word-of-mouth tips and advice on organizing your team, conducting practices, coaching games, and making it fun for you and your players. You'll find this advice formatted in short, quick-reading statements with supporting paragraph information only if you want to read further.

- Section 2: Age-appropriate drills for base running, hitting, fielding, pitching, catching, and more that are suggested by our hometown coaches to help you teach baseball fundamentals in a fun way to your players. Each drill is no more than a two- to three-page read.

- Section 3: Lighthearted and inspirational real-life youth baseball stories as told to us by our coaches and offered for your enjoyment as well as for passing on to your players during pep talks and game conversations.

☐ *Use these coaching ideas as you see fit to develop your own coaching style.*

A good youth baseball coach develops his or her own coaching style by mixing together a set of skills and ideas that he or she thinks will create the best overall experience for the team's players. When we interviewed our hometown hero coaches, we realized that every extraordinary coach creates a magic mix that will be slightly different ... and that is what we intended when we collected their ideas into one book.

You may not necessarily agree with all the advice offered herein or find success with every drill that is suggested. In fact, you will find places in the book where we purposely offered the opposing ideas of two of our coaches. You can decide whether or not you like an idea or think it will benefit your players. We simply offer collective coaching wisdom for your consideration in becoming the best youth baseball coach possible.

With that stated, we do believe that ALL extraordinary youth baseball coaches follow a common set of cardinal rules when they work with kids ... we'd like to offer them to you now.

Ten Cardinal Rules for Extraordinary Youth Baseball Coaching

1. Meet with players' parents before the season starts. Listen to their concerns, share your philosophy and expectations, and ask for their assistance.

2. Learn the rules of the game. Read the rulebook and the guidelines from your specific league or organization to make sure you are teaching the game correctly. Many leagues modify standard rules regarding stealing, leading off, pitching limitations, and substitutions.

3. Try to use ideas and information from as many sources as possible in order to be a better coach. Read other coaching books, attend coaching clinics, and be open to new ideas that could help you coach more effectively.

4. Show up with a plan! Try to involve all kids in all facets of a planned practice. Standing in right field for an hour while everyone else hits is no fun for any player. Whenever possible, run several drills or skill stations concurrently to keep all players involved and interested.

5. Applaud effort and attitude more than performance. Physical errors will happen. If a player has a great attitude and tries hard to make a play, praise him, whether he makes the play or not. For every ten times you speak to your players, nine of them should be praise and applause based on effort and attitude.

6. Encourage any and all kinds of positive teamsmanship between players, from high fives to rally caps and any other form of positive team comradery.

7. You have an obligation to develop the weaker players on your team at least as much (if not more) than the stronger ones. It will pay big dividends by the end of the season for those players _and_ for the team.

8. Do not allow players to criticize teammates, umpires, or opposing players — ever!

9. After every practice and every game, try to find something positive to say about the efforts of several kids, making sure to include each and every player as many times as possible throughout the season. If you put game summaries in the local newspaper, remember to include weaker players and emphasize all aspects of the game, not just home runs.

10. Do anything you can think of to make baseball fun. Remember, these are kids. At this level, learning the game and having fun are always more important and age appropriate than winning games.

1

Coaches' Tips & Advice

This section contains coaches' tips and advice on scores of topics — everything from holding pre-season parent meetings, to developing practice routines, to setting fair and appropriate game line-ups, to dealing with umpires, to tracking pitch counts and maximizing player safety, to motivating and rewarding players — and on and on. We organized this wealth of information into five sections:

- *Organizing Your Team*
- *Conducting Practice*
- *Coaching During Games*
- *Making It Fun*
- *Advice from the Experts*

You can quickly browse through each section and pick up the main ideas by reading the statements next to block bullets ☐ on each page. If you prefer more detail, read the information in paragraphs underneath the block bullets.

Whether you're a rookie coach or a seasoned veteran, we bet you'll find loads of new ideas for promoting excellence, fun, success, sportsmanship, pride, and teamwork while teaching kids baseball!

Organizing Your Team

☐ Learning to Coach Baseball
☐ Communicating With Parents
☐ Recruiting Parent Support
☐ Checklist for Organizing Your Team

One of the most important activities you will perform as a coach during any baseball season is to organize the basic elements of your team. Basic elements include items like learning your league's rules, developing a clear coaching philosophy that you can demonstrate at practices and games, creating a written plan for practices, and determining where you will need assistance from parent volunteers — then communicating all that information to your team's players and their parents. Our hometown hero coaches offer some valuable tips for organizing your team successfully.

Learning to Coach Baseball

Everybody is a rookie coach at some point. We asked our hometown heroes to give us their practical advice on learning to coach baseball.

☐ *Read, observe, and search the Internet for good coaching tips.*

Many of the coaches recommend learning resources such as reading coaching books, observing games, and searching the Internet for youth baseball coaching tips.

Lloyd Rue suggests that new coaches read as much as they can and really understand the general game rules and the specific rules within their own league. Lloyd says the Internet is a great resource. New coaches should search for "coaching" and "youth baseball" and look at some of the many coaching web sites for drills and tips.

Some of **Dennis Dunn's** best learning experiences have come from the numerous baseball schools, clinics and camps that his son has attended over the years. Dennis suggests sitting in on a camp or clinic and taking notes while watching the instructors teach.

Dennis has also learned a lot from watching as much baseball as he can. He watches the pros and colleges, and attends as many youth baseball games as possible. Then he observes the coaches and players to see how they handle different situations. He is also constantly reading and searching for new books and tapes about coaching, always searching for one more tip that can help him improve as a coach.

☐ *Tap into the training resources offered through your league.*

Phil Swan believes that uniformity when training coaches within a league leads to more successful leagues. Everybody hears similar messages and learns similar skills. Phil and another coach within his league help with coach training by using one practice early in the season to conduct a clinic where the players are the instructors. Phil says ...

> *"Why not ... the players usually know the fundamentals better than any parent coaches out there. We use 10- to 12-year-old players from our majors and our upper levels and we have them come out and be our demonstrators and teachers. We conduct a 90-minute practice as a clinic."*

Ryan Callaham encourages any coach, whether they're just starting out or they've been coaching for awhile, to get involved with their league, not just be a coach. Ryan believes that getting involved in your league will allow you to gain insight into what's going on, how to approach issues, and why things are done a certain way.

> *"It has made a world of difference to me … I've seen why things are done the way they are … I also like to think on some form or level that I have helped shape where we're going as a league."*

Communicating With Parents

Letting the parents of kids on your team know what's going on and keeping them updated as the season progresses is a key aspect of any successful season. Here's what our hometown hero coaches recommend to ensure good communication with parents.

☐ *Hold a pre-season parent meeting.*

Many of the coaches we spoke with emphasized the importance of communicating with parents <u>before</u> the season starts to let them know what the coaches' expectations are and to tell them about their coaching styles. **Lloyd Rue** put it nicely:

> *"Preparation, organization, and communication are the keys. I've never coached a baseball season yet where I haven't begun with a parent meeting. I know that at least the appearance of organization … laying out the schedule, the practice and game times, and so on, saves an awful lot of difficulty later on. I like to think of it as the splinter that you don't get if you're wearing gloves. I tell them what my philosophy is and what they should expect with my coaching style, and if they're not seeing that, they need to talk to me or somebody who can come to me…."*

Gilbert Lopez agrees that the parent meeting is critical.

> *"To me, the parent meeting is the most important part of the season because if you don't handle that*

COACH
LLOYD RUE

Helena Babe Ruth Baseball Association
Helena, Montana

Talk about productive … this creative coach provided fifteen drills and just about as many tips from which to choose, including some of the most creative ideas we ran across. Our guess is that the kids on Coach Rue's team don't get bored with the same drills too often!

As far as coaching goes, Lloyd believes that preparation, organization, and communication are key. He is a believer in making sure that everybody understands the coach's philosophy before the start of the season — players and coaches as well as parents. Lloyd points out that it's important to be honest and fair with your team members. If you coach to win and don't like to move players around, then you ought to say that to the team at the beginning of the season. If you coach to rotate players, then that ought to be said as well. We like the straight forward approach to communication that Lloyd Rue practices.

right, it's really not going to work out the rest of the season. I know that from experience. I had one bad year where I didn't have a meeting and I went straight into the practice and it was just chaos. Parents were asking "Why this? Why that? Well, how come my kid is not over here?" Team parent meetings are the first thing that I do before any season starts, whether its spring ball or fall ball."

Gilbert suggests that you call your team players and their parents as soon as you get your team roster. Let the kids know that they are going to be on your team and let the parents know when you are holding your first team meeting. Use that meeting to speak mostly to the parents while the kids go out to the field and throw around some Whiffle® Balls or tennis balls so they don't get hurt.

What do you cover at the parent meeting? Here are a few good thoughts.

☐ Tell parents about your coaching philosophy.

Gilbert Lopez introduces himself and lets parents know what he is all about …

"I'm all about teaching …winning comes second. I mean, I want to win just like the next guy, but I won't do it at all costs. Then I'll also give them my coaching background. I think everybody needs to know what I've done so they feel comfortable that I know what I'm doing."

☐ Set the season's ground rules for parents.

Let the parents know what your rules are about player and parent attitude as well as player effort, focus, and participation.

At his pre-season parent meeting, **Rob Cruz** lets parents know his expectations for them, emphasizing that their main job is to cheer for all the kids. He also emphasizes to them that no one talks to the umpires except the coaches.

> *"I think it's the coach's responsibility to make sure that he treats the umpires fairly and sets a good example for his players and their parents. Good call or bad call, the coach has to move on … and if you do that as a coach, I think the parents will move on, too."*

Colonel John Parker merges his expectations with his philosophy for his teams.

> *"Typically in all the teams, you end up with a couple of kids on one end of the spectrum who are newcomers to the game, and a couple kids on the other end of the spectrum who have been playing for four or five years and are quite experienced. As a coach, I have to try to meld that together to become a baseball team. I try and let the parents understand philosophically where we're trying to go, and that the whole idea of playing this sport is to teach the kids not only the fundamentals of baseball, but to teach them all to give and take and teach and share and put forth a great attitude and effort. They'll make a lot of new friends, they'll enjoy the game of baseball, and they'll learn through this sport how to deal with other things in life."*

Daryl Wasano also makes it a point to tell his parents and players that he doesn't tolerate any display of bad sportsmanship or bad attitude on the field. If his players start to display either of these traits, he immediately pulls them off the field and benches them. By setting this tone with parents and players right away, Daryl says he rarely has any conflicts during a season.

☐ *Explain why parents should not "coach from the stands."*

Several of our hometown hero coaches use the pre-season parent meeting to cover coaching from the stands. **Gilbert**

COACH GILBERT LOPEZ

Round Rock Youth Baseball
Round Rock, Texas

Coach Gilbert Lopez has a pretty simple coaching philosophy … as a manager or as a coach, commit to giving it everything you've got. Coach Lopez likes to spend time getting to know each of his players, their personalities, their skills, and their interests. He spends most of his time working with the players with weaker skills. His reward comes near the end of the season when he sees a player fielding and throwing, who at the beginning of the season couldn't catch a single ball.

Keeping the kids busy at practices is a priority with Coach Lopez. So, he likes to run highly-organized practices with lots of drill stations active simultaneously. Of course, he needs good parent support to help run his practices, and he helps to ensure this by his savvy drafting philosophy … he usually drafts 50% player, 50% parent! Coach Lopez offers more goods tips in "Conducting Practice" in Coaches' Tips & Advice.

**COACH
JON BRAINARD**

**San Dimas
Little League**
San Dimas, California

In his years of mentoring young baseball players, Jon Brainard has developed a very healthy perspective about coaching. As he pointed out to us, most of the kids you'll get on a team will be average or below average baseball players. They're not trying to do anything to hurt you personally, they're not trying to make an error, and they're not trying to strike out. So there's not any reason to get upset with them over their baseball skills … none at all.

Coach Brainard's priority is to make sure his players are enjoying the sport, but also to coach each player to the individual level he shows the coach he is ready to handle. On every team, some kids will be ready for a little more competition and to be pushed a little harder. But, no matter what, a coach's main job is to make sure that every player, even while being competitive, is enjoying himself and learning.

Lopez instructs the parents not to coach from the stands because it can give conflicting information to the players. He uses the example of himself or an assistant coach trying to communicate something to a player such as teaching a player not to run in a particular situation, then a parent starts yelling "run, run, run," which can be very confusing to the player. Basically, Gilbert tells parents to please leave the coaching to the coaches.

"Let us coach. If there's something that you disagree with, if you don't understand why we're teaching something in a certain manner, then take it up with me after the game."

Phil Swan is a big proponent of telling parents that there needs to be one voice on the ball field … the coach. **Ryan Callaham** agrees. As he told us …

"At the first practice every season, I try to make it a point to let the parents know that I understand that it is their son or their daughter … but on the field (whether it's practices or games) their kids belong to me. They are here to cheer for the kids … I don't want anybody coaching from the stands because it puts the kids in an awkward position."

Jon Brainard also urges parents not to coach their kids during a game. He actually gives parents examples of welcome and unwelcome support. He encourages parents to motivate their kids with statements like, "Hit the ball hard!" or "Get a hit here!" But, he discourages parents from yelling out statements like, "Get your elbow up!" or "Get your knees bent!" or "Why did you swing at that pitch?"

☐ *Talk with parents about player safety.*

This tip is especially important for coaches of young players. **Gilbert Lopez** suggests that coaches use the pre-season parent meeting to cover some issues on player safety. He explains that you get a lot of parents who want their young child to begin immediately playing the key field positions like pitcher, first base, second base, third base, and so on. But Gilbert reminds us that putting inexperienced or immature players into these key positions can be an unsafe coaching decision. He calls these types of players "sand angels."

> *"Dealing with T-ballers, you see a lot of what we call 'sand angels' … you know, those are the kids that play in the dirt or sand or grass. They're not paying attention to what is going on with the game … they're just in their own little world. Normally, when I have sand angels on my team, I position them in the outfield. Then I make sure to let the parents know why they are out there. I can't put a player in a position where he or she might get hurt by a runner or a fast-moving ball because of not paying attention. I've seen kids get hit in the face and I've seen kids get hit in the head because they weren't paying attention to what was going on. I wouldn't want that to happen to any of my kids."*

At the parent meeting, Gilbert makes it clear that he is not going to put players in positions where he thinks they will be unsafe. Instead, he puts each player into a position that he thinks they can handle. When he can teach them to pay attention and to watch the baseball everywhere it goes, he'll move them into the infield and give them more of that kind of playing time.

☐ *Tell parents to come to you at appropriate times with questions or concerns.*

Colonel Parker emphasizes to his team's parents that they should feel comfortable approaching him to talk about any issue or concern they may have. But, too many times he's watched a parent discuss a situation with his or her child present or make comments in front of a child that should be discussed adult to adult. Coach Colonel (as many of his players call him) also likes to remind parents that various coaches won't necessarily do everything the same way, or the way a particular parent might have chosen, but if

COACH BRIG SORBER

**Okemos
Baseball/Softball Club**
Okemos, Michigan

We agree with Brig Sorber that youth baseball is all about fun and fundamentals. Coach Sorber believes that if you can keep the season fun as well as teach the players something, they will continue to come back and play again. In the Okemos Baseball/ Softball Club, the coaches are all encouraged to develop their players on many levels — making sure they are focused and their attitudes are on straight, that they're supporting each other, and that there is teaching going on for the most gifted player as well as the most challenged player.

Brig makes sure that his team parents understand this philosophy and how many balls a coach is usually trying to juggle in order to give the kids a good experience. That helps him to emphasize why it's important to have as many parent volunteers with positive attitudes as possible. We salute this hometown hero for his great coaching attitude!

a parent feels there is an issue they should bring it up for discussion.

As with many of the coaches we spoke with, Colonel Parker advises that, during practices and games, coaching calls need to be left in the hands of the coaching staff. **Ryan Callaham** agrees with the Colonel.

> *"If parents have a problem with the way their child is being coached or where he is being played, or if they have a question about the team, they are more than welcome to come to me to discuss it. But, please, don't ask me during the game. Instead, contact me when the kids aren't around."*

☐ *Suggest to parents what type of equipment they should get for their kids.*

Every year, **Gilbert Lopez** gets questions from parents about the kind of bat or other playing equipment they should get for their child. He tells parents that a good tactic for determining when the bat is too heavy is to have their child hold the bat out in front of their body using just one arm, with their hand grasping the very end of the bat. If they can't hold the bat steady for at least five seconds, then it's too heavy for them.

JC Petersen always tells parents to try getting their children used baseball gloves because they are broken in and they bend so much better. He also lets parents and players know about his rule for bringing special baseball equipment (like catcher's equipment or a first baseman's mitt or a donut) to practice. JC makes it clear that anything brought to a practice "belongs" to the team during that practice, so anyone on the team can use it.

☐ *Put important information in writing.*

Brig Sorber likes to communicate his coaching thoughts and rules to parents in a letter. He does this as soon as he gets his roster for the season. He explains his goals for the team and emphasizes his team rules. For example, Brig takes this opportunity to let the parents know that he, as the coach, will be the only one speaking with the umpire during games.

Monie Duran is a big advocate of both coaches and parents knowing the basic rules of the game, especially because there are specific rules for each level of baseball. She likes to put out a newsletter for the parents specifying the rules for the level of baseball that she's coaching. In Monie's case, since she coaches primarily T-ball, she also wants parents to know that there is no keeping score at that age level and that she will have all players on the team play all the positions. Monie reminds the parents not to coach the kids from the stands and offer them only positive comments.

Recruiting Parent Support

Almost every team can always use parents to volunteer as assistant coaches or to support the team in other ways.

☐ *Use the parent meeting to recruit volunteers.*

Gilbert Lopez uses the parent meeting to ask for all the help he can get. Even if he already has three or four coaches, he always tries to get all the parents involved as much as possible.

Coaching isn't the only place that Gilbert asks for help. He also asks for volunteers to take responsibility for organizing the team snacks to be distributed after the game, announcing the game, keeping score, and helping get kids ready for their at bats. If a parent is not able to help at practices or games, Gilbert asks them if they can organize an outing for the team, an end-of-season party, or whatever else the parent would like to do.

"If you make parents feel like a part of the team, they will bend over backwards to make it a success."

Rob Cruz

☐ Give parents a specific supporting role for their player.

Jon Brainard gets his team's parents involved in a very creative way. At the beginning of the year, he creates a goals sheet for every player on his team. Jon creates a list of up to ten goals for each player such as "participate in making an out on defense," "get a hit," "get a double," "hit a fly ball," and so on. He tries to make the goals attainable for everyone, listing things that he as a coach can control (like getting a player to steal at least once during the season). Then Jon gives each child's sheet to his or her parent at the first team meeting and charges the parents with keeping track of the goals for their child.

This gets all the parents involved, and most of the parents willingly participate in the activity. Jon has also seen parents send an older brother or sister to keep track of a player's goals when the parent couldn't make a game.

> *"I've had kids that make a play on the field and then shout back to the stands to their parents, "Did you get that?" They like to make sure that their goals are being recorded!"*

As incentive to reach the goals, Jon makes tokens on his computer (you can also buy stickers) and he awards the tokens for goal achievement to players at several points in the season. The tokens can be traded in for quarters (provided by the coach) to use in the arcade at the local pizza parlor.

☐ Use the league volunteer recruiting process.

Bob Karol says that his league also solicits parent volunteers at the league level to coordinate the Opening Day Parade, the Closing Day Picnic, securing team sponsorships, and so on.

"Our attitude is always anybody who wants to coach, let them coach. Especially in a situation where there are lots of parents who may travel for business and can't get to every game, it helps to have backup coaches and other assistants."

☐ **Promote consistency in volunteer style and philosophy.**

Lloyd Rue cautions, however, that volunteer coaches should have a little consistency in style and philosophy. Lloyd suggests the following:

"If parents are going to help, I want them to start helping at the beginning of the season. One time I had a parent who came in to help in the middle of the season and he had some very different coaching philosophies from me. He volunteered as a coach for just a few games and then he left. That created a real problem. So, I prefer to do my parent volunteer recruiting at the beginning of the season."

Checklist for Organizing Your Team

Pre-season organization is a critical element of a solid start to any season. Therefore, we've provided you with a summary checklist of tips recommended by our hometown hero coaches (as well as a few we added ourselves!)

Learning to Coach Baseball

☐ *Read, observe, and search the Internet for good coaching tips.*

☐ *Tap into the training resources offered through your league.*

checklist continued on next page

COACH
BOB KAROL

Wayland Baseball & Softball Association
Wayland, Massachusetts

Coach Bob Karol believes his primary role in coaching kids is teaching them how to be good human beings ... that is, being a good sport, handling success as well as failure, being part of the team, honesty, and improving yourself ... all the things that they'll encounter as adults.

Bob Karol structures his practices so that he can pay special attention to the weaker players. During a practice, he'll hit 50 ground balls to his starting shortstop, but 150 ground balls to the player who can't catch the ball at all.

Bob also tries to remember to look at the outcome of any game from the eyes of the players. For most kids, winning is not all that important in the long run. Being with their friends and having fun is what's important. Kids very quickly get over that two to one loss as soon as the coach says, "Anybody want ice cream?"

(checklist continued)

Communicating With Parents

☐ *Hold a pre-season parent meeting. At that meeting:*

___ *Tell parents about your coaching philosophy*
___ *Set the season's ground rules for parents*
___ *Explain why parents should not "coach from the stands"*
___ *Talk with parents about player safety*
___ *Tell parents to come to you at appropriate times with questions or concerns*
___ *Suggest to parents what type of equipment they should get for their kids*
___ *Recruit parent volunteers*

☐ *Put important information in writing.*

Recruiting Parent Support

☐ *Give parents a specific supporting role for their player.*
☐ *Use the league volunteer recruiting process.*
☐ *Promote consistency in volunteer style and philosophy.*

Before the First Practice

☐ *Check out your team's equipment (usually provided by the league) to make sure it's complete and in good shape so it can be used safely and effectively in your practices and games.*

☐ *Check out the practice field you've been assigned and make sure you communicate driving directions to that field to all your team's parents. When you give directions, use the proper name of the school or park where you will practice, not the league "nickname" for that field. Otherwise, some parents will be confused, especially those who are new to the league.*

☐ *Set up an email list for your team so you can quickly and efficiently distribute information like directions to fields or changes in the practice schedule.*

"Since I've started doing a parent meeting, my seasons have just been awesome, things go very smoothly, and you get a lot of respect."

Gilbert Lopez

Conducting Practice

☐ Planning Practices
☐ The First Practice
☐ Practice Routines
☐ Using Assistants
☐ Using Equipment Creatively
☐ Working with Younger Kids
☐ Specific Fundamentals Work

Our hometown heroes gave us loads of advice on conducting youth baseball practices. We have intentionally included as many different thoughts as possible in this section, even conflicting ideas in some cases, as we understand that not everyone agrees on all the same strategies for success with young players. You should browse through this section, then use those suggestions that seem to best fit with your own personal coaching style. The point to remember is that all these ideas have worked in one way or another for at least one of our hometown hero coaches.

Planning Practices

Thorough planning and organization are the keys to success when teaching kids baseball. Here are some great suggestions and strategies to try with your team.

☐ *Go in with a written plan.*

Many of the coaches we spoke with recommended preparing for practice by creating a written plan.

Colonel Parker summarized it nicely …

"The key is organization, without a doubt. I come to every practice with a written plan. You've got to think about what you are going to do with these kids. You can't just get there and say, 'O.K., today we're going to do this.' You've got to know what you want to do with your infielders, what you want to do with your outfielders, what you want to do with your batting, and so on.

Some days you're batting and some days you're bunting. Some days you're doing a lot of throws to first base and other days you're going to work on outfielders relaying throws to the infield or on base running. To be a successful coach takes some forethought before you go into practice.

Think about what you want to accomplish and how you want to divide up your kids. Think about what they need to be doing. Your plan doesn't have to be three pages long; typically mine are only a page long."

Dennis Dunn likes to have a written plan for practices too, as does **John Gentile**. John says his plans are never fancy. Sometimes they're just notes jotted on a piece of paper. Both coaches think that a written plan is critical for keeping things moving and keeping the kids focused and interested.

☐ *Prep your assistant coaches on your plan.*

Colonel Parker always makes it a point to share his practice plan with his assistant coaches while the kids are loosening up and throwing baseballs to each other. As many of our coaches do, Coach Parker likes to work his players through "fundamentals" stations, and he asks an assistant coach to manage each station.

"Mike, I want you to take these guys to the cages and these are the first four players I want to go with you. David, I want you to take these five outfielders

and have them all practice going to the right. I'm going to take the infielders and I'm going to work on bunting. Then, when it's time to switch, I want the guys who are in the batting cages to come over here and we're going to be working on pitchers covering home with catchers. The infielders will go over to the batting cages and the outfielders will go to base running."

Coach Parker stresses that this type of organization takes time to plan, but there's a big payoff because you end up with productive practices where kids are doing a lot more than just scrimmaging or throwing the ball around for a couple of hours.

☐ *Keep practices short.*

Practices should be no more than two hours in length, and shorter for younger kids. **John Mangieri** usually makes his practices only 60 to 90 minutes in duration. For younger kids, he would rather have more one-hour practices than fewer long practices. Then, as the kids get older, the length of each practice can be increased.

☐ *Don't over-schedule games instead of practices.*

Bob Karol encourages coaches and leagues to make sure they have enough practice time, because you can teach the kids sportsmanship and teamwork in games, but skills need to be taught in practices. If kids are begging for "game time," you can hold scrimmages at the end of many practices. Scrimmages are great in practice because they allow you to play in a game format, but stop and teach when you need to do so. Scrimmages also give kids who might want to try pitching or catching an opportunity to do so without the pressure of a real game where you might be setting them up to fail.

"COACH COLONEL"
JOHN PARKER

Dixie Youth Baseball
Hilton Head Island,
South Carolina

When we interviewed "Coach Colonel," as many of his players call him, we thought his coaching philosophy was right on the money. Colonel Parker said, "I really focus on two things … attitude and effort. It's really important for young kids to learn that baseball and life kind of go hand-in-hand. If you have a great attitude and you give 100%, everything will work out just fine."

Although the Colonel has coached teams of 9- and 10-year-olds to become Dixie Youth Baseball League 9-10 World Series Champions, he tells us that the real reward isn't winning. "The real reward is when you see those kids a year or two later, and they come up to you and tell you what a good time they had last year! Getting kids involved and liking the game plus knowing that they've had a good time and grown through their experience … that's the reward."

The First Practice

There are a few things that are unique about the first practice of a season. The first practice offers coaches the opportunity to set the tone for the season and to motivate players to work hard. Our hometown heroes offer these suggestions for conducting that first practice.

☐ *Set the tone for your team.*

At his first practice each season, before he and the kids go over any elements of the game, **Mike Miselis** likes to sit everybody in a circle and explain about working hard. Coach Miselis lets his players know that as long as they give him 110%, he will guarantee that they will have a good season and that they will learn something.

Rod Hudson believes in setting the tone for his team by keeping a positive demeanor at all times. He understands that, especially at the first practice, coaches are "on display." Parents and players are checking the coach out to see what type of coaching style he or she will use. The first practice is the most important time to set the tone by providing lots of positive and encouraging comments like, "Great catch!" and "Nice throw!"

Coach Hudson also uses the first practice to get parents involved with the team's effort. Here are some of his tips:

·   At the first practice, introduce yourself to both the kids *and* their parents. It's important that each player as well as his or her parents feel welcomed and part of a positive group.

·   While the parents are still there (or when they come to pick up their child at the end of the practice), explain how their participation is also required for the success of the team. Coach Hudson suggests that the first practice is a great time to seek out volunteers for snack/drink coordinator, score keeper, or additional assistant coaches.

Provide parents and players with practice and game schedules if available and explain the importance of getting to practices and games on time. Coach Hudson recommends that his players be at the field at least 30 minutes prior to any game. He also explains that all players are required to be at practice, plus he asks that either a player or his parent call him if the player plans to be late or miss either a practice or a game.

☐ *Show your enthusiasm for baseball — it's contagious!*

The first practice talk, by Coach **Brig Sorber's** account, is the most important thing he does all season. Before any drills are run or any balls are thrown, Coach Sorber sits his players down on the bench and speaks with them about motivation and teamwork. Here's his creative approach and a great first team speech ...

> *"I take an old leather ball out of my bag and I just take a big whiff of it. Then I pass the ball around and ask the players to do the same. As if they aren't looking at me funny by then, I ask them to rub their gloves all over their faces and smell them too. I say to them ... now, that's baseball! They all laugh at that ... some think it's funny and some think it's kind of weird. Then, I tell them that everybody on this team is a little bit different, but that we're ALL going to get better together. I'm very strict about this. I make sure they understand that if anybody laughs or makes fun of somebody else for his or her talents or for taking a risk and not doing something right, then that person will sit. Everybody is going to go a hundred and ten miles an hour here and everybody's going to fail at something during the season. We're not here to win games ... we're here to get better. And we're going to get better as a team."*

Coach Sorber also talks to his players about having a positive attitude on the ballfield — supporting each other and not "trash talking." He lets them know that if they

COACH ROD HUDSON

Germantown Athletic Club
Germantown, Maryland

Listening to Rod Hudson coach his players on the baseball field is a motivating experience. A stickler for keeping a positive demeanor at all times, Coach Hudson knows that his players (and their parents) are watching every move he makes and listening carefully for his words of encouragement to the team.

Coach Hudson is a master at building team camaraderie with his creative ideas for motivating players. From creating fun player nicknames to a quick team cap slap for a great play, Rod knows how to make his players feel special. Read about all his other great tips in "Making It Fun" in Coaches' Tips & Advice.

Coach Hudson strives to develop a positive relationship with all his players, even phoning a player just to ask how his or her everyday life is going — schoolwork, playing with the team, and so on. Our hats go off to Coach Hudson for keeping the word "positive" in his coaching style at all times.

want to impress him, then they should look for ways to be a team player and help each other out.

> *"When you're up at bat and the catcher's coming up to get in position, grab the catcher's mask and hand it to the catcher ... impress me that way."*

Rod Hudson always ends his first practice (and all of his other practices for that matter) by demonstrating his spirit and enthusiasm for the game to his players.

> *"I conclude my first practice with a huddle chant where everyone gathers together and places a hand in the center of the huddle. Then, I lead the team chant by yelling, 'On 3 everyone ... 1-2-3 GO BIG RED!' ... or blue, or the team's nickname. As the season progresses, I ask each player to take a turn leading us in the huddle chant."*

Coach Hudson makes it a point to do this same chant at the end of every practice and before and after every game. He also uses it between innings to get a little spirit going.

Practice Routines

Most of our hometown hero coaches have certain routines or patterns for the way that they like to set up practices. Some believe in running team-based drills while others think that station drills where kids are broken into small groups are best. Some work on fundamentals with the whole team and others like to focus mostly on the pitchers or catchers. Whatever routines they use, we found that all these coaches came to practices with an organized plan that included focused skills activities as well as a little fun and motivation for playing the sport of baseball. Browse through these ideas and incorporate those that you agree with into your own practice routines.

☐ *Hold short practices that keep the kids moving.*

JC Petersen usually starts his practices with a base running drill of some sort, then he has the team do something short and specific about a problem or a weakness they had during a previous game or practice.

> *"I generally never start with anything where the kids are going to stand around. Instead, I do really short drills, maybe ten minutes each. I like to use simple, multi-skill drills. By that, I mean if we're doing a defensive drill in the infield, I'm also going to have a base runner or two involved in that drill.*
>
> *I also do tons of running stuff. They love it. You can do a hundred things in baseball related to running, whether it's leading off or rounding a base, or something else. Running is something that all the kids can get into right away so they're all moving."*

JC tries to end his practices with at least 30 minutes of "quick games," where he divides the kids into two teams of equal numbers, then he'll pitch and get one player to catch. If there are enough kids at practice, JC also likes to use a player as the first base coach instead of an adult. During "quick games," Coach Petersen doesn't use any outfield, just the infield positions. If someone hits a ball to the outfield, JC just gives them a few bases, maybe to second or third. The play is very fast, so the kids quickly get into a game-like activity where they are using all their skills.

JC likes his practices to go no longer than 90 minutes. Since he works with 9-, 10-, and 11-year-olds, he doesn't think you can hold kids' attention much longer than that.

COACH DARYL WASANO

Oceanside American Little League
Oceanside, California

We found Daryl Wasano on television. After watching the elegant way he handled his coaching duties at the regional finals of the Little League® World Series Championships, we were convinced that Coach Wasano was a hometown coaching hero with whom we needed to speak.

Daryl's firm belief is that all players and coaches must bring a positive attitude to the ball field every time, displaying good sportsmanship in all situations. Coach Wasano teaches his players to be gracious winners as well as gracious losers.

Daryl considers himself a strict coach as far as attitude goes. He believes that you can teach a player with a good attitude to play any position on the ball field, but a player with a bad attitude is uncoachable. We loved the way he put his philosophy to us, "I coach "we" teams, not "me" and "I" teams." ESPN loved it too ... they recognized Daryl as a top all-time exhibitor of good sportsmanship!

☐ *Do station drills and end with a base race.*

Here's how **Gilbert Lopez** runs his practices ...

"Keeping the kids busy in practice is a big deal for me. Organization is a big deal for me. I don't like to have a practice where I've got kids goofing around because there's nothing going on.

I try to stay away from a lot of team drills. Instead, I do station drills ... you know, Station #1, Station #2, Station #3, and so on.

Usually, at the end of practice, I run a base race, where I line up half my kids at home plate and half of them at second base. Then, on my signal, they run in a relay fashion, each player running all the way around the bases once and tagging up with their relay team until all the players have run. The relay team at home plate races against the relay team at second base to see who can finish first. I finish my practice off with that, and the kids love it."

Dennis Dunn also runs this relay race at the end of some of his practices (see the "Base Running Relay Race" Drill.) Since he works with older players (12-14 years old), Dennis makes the team who loses pick up all the field equipment, pack it up, and walk it back from the field to the coach's car!

☐ *Use a set practice format with routine drills.*

Daryl Wasano works with a number of all-star teams and uses a set practice format with routine drills from start to finish. He feels that repetition is the key with his players. Daryl tries to make his practices two hours long with everybody participating, so there is no player who is left out of a drill and there's nobody standing around. If he has 12 or 13 players show up for practice, he'll send some out to the outfield for drills and keep some in the infield, then switch them as soon as the drills are done. If he has more players than infield positions during a drill, Daryl places two players in some positions so they can alternate playing that position.

Everybody practices at a lot of different positions. Then, if something happens to a player during a game, Daryl's team has someone to back up that player's position if need be.

Since Daryl feels that defense is the key to a strong team, he likes to work on defensive drills in the three to four weeks before a season starts, so his players get lots of repetition in fundamentals. Then, about a week before the team will play their first game, he switches his practices to hitting drills. "I kind of dangle the carrot of hitting practice in front of the players," he says.

☐ *Have younger players learn by evaluating each other.*

Lloyd Rue uses the players on his teams as teachers and models for each other.

> *"We'll have the younger kids watch each other perform a drill, then evaluate each other in a positive fashion. Sometimes we ask the kids to rate the other players on a scale from 1 to 10 on skills like throwing speed, mechanics, and so on."*

In general, Lloyd tries to do his practices in "sets of three." In other words, he uses the same sets of drills for three practices, then he switches them around. Repeating drills for multiple practices cuts down on the time it takes to get the kids organized for each drill.

Lloyd says that, as far as drills go, he's thrown out as many as he has kept.

> *"I always try not to confuse the organization of the drill with what I'm really trying to accomplish, which is building a specific skill. If I try a drill and it*

HOMETOWN HERO PROFILE

COACH
MIKE MISELIS

**Bayonne Cal
Ripken Baseball**
Bayonne, New Jersey

Mike Miselis is a 25-year coaching veteran and knows firsthand the rewards of a positive coaching experience. "It's the best feeling in the world to see a kid who you've coached several years later. Now they're all grown up, maybe even married and with kids of their own, and they come up to you and shake your hand and tell you how you were such a positive influence and an important part of their growing up."

Part of building those lasting memories for every player, as Coach Miselis points out, is to stress to your players that "it's the little things that count." Home runs are nice and they're exciting, but home runs are not going to win a game most of the time. It's the little contributions that each team member makes when playing games ... backing up, playing smart, showing leadership on the field, and so on. That's Coach Miselis' secret to building winning teams.

doesn't work, then I bag it for that practice and try it again the next practice. I like to try a new drill three times. If it still isn't working then I bag that drill for good and go on to another drill."

☐ Work on real plays and use variations of the same drill.

John Mangieri likes to work on real plays at his team practices; working on the cutoff man, turning double plays, and so on. He doesn't believe in drilling to the point of boredom, especially with younger players who have short attention spans. When he does use drills, John likes to keep them short and moving quickly. To keep consistency in the fundamentals being practiced, John points out that the same goals can often be accomplished by using different variations of one drill.

☐ Turn your drills into games with incentives and rewards.

Mike Miselis knows that making anything into a game will help kids be more motivated to do it. He tries to add something new at every practice, not only for the kids, but for the coaches, because the same drills can get rather boring after awhile.

Offering incentives and rewards for good performance or sportsmanship also works well. **John Mangieri** likes to promise his players a game of "Workup" (see Coaches' Favorite Drills) at the end of practice if they concentrate really hard on performing the drills. Even little incentives like candy or points towards prizes work well for keeping kids motivated. See "Making It Fun" in Coaches' Tips & Advice for more ideas.

☐ *Use the last few minutes of practice to wrap up and take questions.*

John Gentile suggests that all coaches use the last few minutes of practice to sit down with the players and summarize what was covered that day. Ask the kids some questions about what they learned. For example, "How do you catch a fly ball?" or "How do you catch a grounder?" Let the players answer your questions. Then ask them if they have any questions at that point.

☐ *Help players to learn the game rules.*

Players who join your team come from different experiences and backgrounds, so it's up to you to help assure that they all know the rules consistently.

Lloyd Rue likes to use the first three or four practices to cover rules that are commonly misunderstood or misapplied by his players. Lloyd picks out seven to ten rules for each practice, things they might run into during a game, and he hands them a sheet with information on each rule. He briefly goes over the rules, then he lets the players have a couple of days to think about those rules and share them with their parents. At the end of the next practice, Coach Rue gives the players a quick verbal quiz on those rules.

☐ *Take time to plan a dynamic practice.*

Phil Swan thinks that one of the most difficult challenges for a youth coach is developing a dynamic baseball practice composed of the right drills that is still fun for kids. Phil believes in a 90-minute practice for kids because he thinks that is the optimal amount of time for holding most kids' attention.

Phil thinks that the order of the drills in a practice is incredibly important for a couple of reasons: (1) the safety factor involved with moving and working certain muscles;

HOMETOWN HERO PROFILE

COACH JOHN GENTILE

New Castle Little League
New Castle, Delaware

When we interviewed John Gentile, we loved the story he relayed to us about attitude. After Coach Gentile's team lost the championship game, a young player on his team came up to John's wife and said, "They might have won the championship, but nobody had as much fun as we did this year." That's exactly the attitude we love to hear expressed from young players and a good reason to include John Gentile as one of our hometown hero coaches.

Coach Gentile offered other good advice like going into each practice with a written plan so you don't waste your own time as well as the kids' time. It also helps you to gauge whether or not you are interjecting enough fun in your practice routines ... a few serious baseball drills mixed in with a few drills that are mostly for team building or fun. We think Coach Gentile's philosophy is right on the mark!

and, (2) the efficiency factor for maximum effectiveness out of the practice. If the drills in your practice are organized in the right way, you can do a lot in 90 minutes while still keeping kids very engaged.

Phil has worked with a fellow coach to develop "Ted and Phil's Dynamic 90-Minute Baseball Practice." We modified his practice sequence to make it more generic for all coaches.

<u>Adapted Version of</u>
<u>Ted and Phil's Dynamic 90-Minute Baseball Practice</u>
(you can customize this to fit your needs)

Time (minutes)	Activity	Details
10	Stretching exercises	Warm up all parts of body including neck, shoulders, arms, wrists, waist, legs, ankles, abdominals
3	Coach's briefing	Provide players with a brief overview of today's practice and goals to achieve
15	Base running drills	For example, sliding, stealing, running from home to first base, running from third base to home
15	Throwing and pitching drills	For example, cutoff throws, pitching mechanics
15	Fielding drills	For example, practice fielding grounders, catching fly balls, pickle
15	Hitting drills	For example, practice hitting mechanics, bunts
15	Game simulation activities	For example, team scrimmaging activities, workup games and full team drills
2	Coach's debriefing	Review practice and goals achieved, areas to work on as a team and individuals, reminders of next practice/ game time and place

The specific drills used during a 90-minute practice can either be taken from this book or from a variety of other resources. This basic practice sequence, however, can work well for players of ages nine and older.

For an alternate viewpoint on practice duration and activities for players of various ages, see Bob Bigelow's information in "Adapting a Coaching Style for Children" in Coaches' Tips & Advice.

Using Assistants

Almost all of our hometown hero coaches are big proponents of using as many assistants as possible to help with practices. Here are some of their tips for using assistants wisely.

☐ *Get as many parents involved as you can.*

Jeff Mathis likes to get as many parents involved as possible and he does much of his recruiting at the pre-season parents' meeting. Coach Mathis tells parents that he doesn't consider himself a cheap baby sitter, so he expects them to get involved and help with the team. One thing that Jeff works to avoid, however, is a parent working too closely with his own child at practice.

> *"I want them working with another kid ... not their own, because a lot of times parents will think that their own child should be doing better than he or she is doing ... it puts too much pressure on the kids. So, I try to get them working with the other players if possible."*

Rob Cruz, on the other hand, recommends the first day of practice for recruiting assistants because that's when all the parents are there. They want to see what the coach is like and hear what the coach has to say, so it's the ideal time to get them involved. If you don't get them to volunteer on that day, you're not likely to get them to come back and help out later in the season.

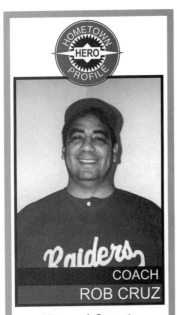

HERO
HOMETOWN PROFILE

COACH
ROB CRUZ

**Howard County
Youth Program**
Ellicott City, Maryland

Among his most important goals for his team of 10-year-olds is the commitment by Rob Cruz to make sure that every player feels like he or she is an important part of the team. So, Coach Cruz emphasizes equal playing time for everyone. He wants to make sure that by the end of the season, his players are all better prepared to play the game of baseball.

Coach Cruz also likes to put players into field positions where he knows they will have some success. He's not an advocate of putting each player into every field position. It's often a matter of safety, as Rob states, to make sure that the fundamental skills are present before you place a player into a key position. At the same time, though, Rob will make an effort to get as many players as he can to both outfield and infield positions in a game. Rob's thoughtful attitude scores points with us!

☐ *Match your assistant's activities with his or her skill level.*

Colonel Parker believes that the more coaches you can have, regardless of their skill sets, the better off you are because skills can be practiced with smaller groups of kids. For example, you can use a volunteer who doesn't understand much about the game to toss underhand to a small group of kids who are practicing bunt fundamentals. Then you can have an assistant who knows more about baseball work with a group of kids in the infield covering bunts. You can use a third assistant, who is fairly new to the sport, but has the strength to hit or throw, to send pop flies out to a group of outfielders. The smaller you can make the player groups, the more focused and active your practice will be and the more the kids are going to enjoy it.

☐ *Teach assistants the fundamentals too.*

Tom Sutton knows that it is important to make sure your assistants have been shown a drill before they are asked to implement it with the team's players. You can give your assistants something that isn't hard to do and show them how to do it properly. Then, once they understand the basics, both the assistants and the players can enjoy the practice and you can move on to another group of players at another station. With three or four assistants each coordinating a drill station, you can move around to each station and make sure that everything is going well. This strategy also keeps the practice flowing.

Rob Cruz likes to pair up volunteer parents with his official assistant coaches so they see how to properly teach the fundamentals. Coach Cruz also lets assistants and volunteers coach bases during scrimmages. It gets them really involved and allows them to have input to the team.

❑ *Mentor younger players with older players.*

An interesting and creative tip from **Bill Sandry** is to have older players mentor younger ones. Coach Sandry suggests contacting the coach of a team in your league with older kids (maybe 11- to 12-year-olds for mentoring 9- to 10-year-olds) and ask him if you could hold a practice together.

> *"We had the older players be demonstrators through all of our drills, then we asked them to mentor the younger kids. It was really great because the younger kids really looked up to the older kids, even though they weren't much bigger than them. They couldn't believe what kids who were just a few inches taller than them could do. The older kids felt like they were pretty special because they were actually getting to coach. I had a couple of kids on my team who hardly spoke at all, but they talked more in that one hour than they probably talked all year. Putting older kids in a spot where they are teaching younger kids is good for both."*

❑ *Be organized and in charge — everybody likes a leader.*

When you use assistants, it is important to remember that you are still in charge of the overall practice plan. **Rob Cruz** believes that everybody likes a leader. He makes sure that everybody understands that he is the manager of a team, even though he openly asks for input from the parents of his players. He likes it when parents tell him what is on their minds or gives him suggestions, because no coach has all the answers. However, Coach Cruz also knows that he is ultimately responsible for the organization of practices, game strategies, and a productive season for his players.

Using Equipment Creatively

Often times, coaches don't think of using equipment that is meant for other sports (like tennis balls or jump ropes) in a baseball practice. Coaches of older players can also make creative use of any special equipment that the league has available for use with its younger-age teams (like batting tees or pitching machines.) Here are some tips from our hometown heroes on the creative use of sports equipment to assist you with practices.

☐ *Use a pitching machine for infield and outfield practice.*

Both **Dennis Nickerson** and **Russ Thompson** suggest using a pitching machine for outfield practice. As Dennis told us ...

> *"I've started using a pitching machine for outfield flies. You can only hit so many fly balls to the kids. But with the pitching machine, you can do it for hours, not wear anybody out, and they're all good balls to catch and learn from."*

Coach Nickerson has even used the machine from third base to first base to work with the first baseman on digging a ball out of the dirt.

Coach Thompson sometimes sets up two lines of outfielders and uses the pitching machine to shoot fly balls between them. This maneuver forces the outfielders to talk to each other ... who is going to call for the ball, who is going to back that player up, and so on. Russ says the younger kids really get a lot out of this one because they learn to communicate.

Russ notes that running the pitching machine is a perfect job for a parent assistant who might not know a lot about baseball but is willing to help with practices.

☐ *Use tennis balls for drills.*

This tip works nicely for younger players as well as for players who may be afraid of the hard baseball. **Phil Swan** was among the coaches who mentioned this idea. Coach Swan uses tennis balls for a variety of drills including teaching kids to catch fly balls.

> *"It forces them to catch the ball with two hands and in the web of the glove. You just can't catch a tennis ball in the palm of your hand. You know, Walt Weiss, who was a shortstop for the Colorado Rockies and the Oakland Athletics was a huge believer in tennis balls. He always said that there isn't a major leaguer out there who hasn't been afraid of the ball at one time or another."*

Coach Swan knows that using tennis balls allows a player's muscle memory to develop without his or her fear factor kicking in. He also notes that it is actually more difficult to perform some baseball skills correctly with a tennis ball. The kids are relieved when they switch to the hard ball to find out how much easier it is compared to a tennis ball. This gives them a sense of success and achievement.

☐ *Use a batting tee to teach hitting at all levels.*

Everybody remembers using a batting tee for coaching their very young players. But, **Russ Thompson** notes that the batting tee can be extremely useful even though players have moved beyond the T-ball level. The tee is great because kids tend to get away from fundamentals, and when you're a coach and throwing pitches during batting practice, it's difficult to also see what a player is doing wrong. Coach Thompson notes that if you get players batting off a tee then you can stand back and really break down their swing and see what they're doing wrong and what they're doing right. Lots of times, you can ask them to concentrate on a few simple things to improve their swing. By hitting off a tee they can also feel it themselves.

COACH PHIL SWAN

North Boulder Little League
Boulder, Colorado

Coach Swan is not only a master of coaching young players, but he also helps his league by training coaches. Phil's years of experience have led him to conclude that it is often difficult for a coach to develop a dynamic baseball practice that teaches good fundamentals in all areas, but keeps the kids interested for the duration of the practice session. So, he and another coach in his league have developed a dynamic 90-minute baseball practice (see "Practice Routines" in Coaches' Tips & Advice), incorporating drills from several sources, that gives the kids a chance to stretch, run, throw, catch, hit, simulate game plays, and also provides time for players' briefing and debriefing.

Phil offers his structured approach to other coaches as a way to help them promote safety, efficiency, effectiveness, and fun for their players. Way to go, Phil, for being a mentor to the young and the … um … not so young!!

❑ *Practice batting with thundersticks, golf balls, soccer balls, and more.*

Sometimes using balls meant for other sports during batting practice can be fun and educational. **Phil Swan** likes to help his players strengthen their back swings by having them try to hit softballs and deflated soccer balls. He also uses a device called the "thunderstick" that is advertised in most baseball magazines. It's a very thin stick that is round and weighted the same as a baseball bat. Coach Swan has his players hit a set of miniature plastic golf balls using the thunder stick to teach them eye-hand coordination.

Working with Younger Kids

Holding a practice with younger kids, say between the ages of five and seven, can be a special challenge. Their attention spans are usually quite short and many of them still lack the proper motor skills to move swiftly and smoothly through complex drills. A few of our hometown hero coaches provided us with tips specifically for working with younger players.

❑ *Keep practices very basic.*

Monie Duran has spent a lot of time coaching the youngest players and has developed a lot of good strategies for working with them.

> "The first day of practice we have a discussion about the field. We start by learning the diamond, the bases, the outfield, and what all the positions mean. Then we practice running to each base so the players get familiar with the bases and the correct way to run around them."

☐ *Use tennis balls for throwing and catching.*

Jeff Mathis, another coach who has worked with young players, thinks that the most important skill you can teach young players is not to be afraid of the ball. He uses tennis balls instead of hard baseballs or even softer T-ball "flex" balls.

> *"I actually had an assistant coach throw a tennis ball to hit me so I could show the kids that it doesn't hurt."*

Monie Duran also starts working on throwing and fielding skills with a tennis ball because she knows that a lot of young players have never even caught a ball before. She doesn't want them to get hurt or become afraid of the ball. For batting practice, Monie recommends using a Whiffle® Ball. Then, she switches to using a T-ball "flex" ball for batting during the actual games.

Coach Duran also starts the season's practices off having her players practice catching and fielding skills without using their gloves. She lets them concentrate on learning the basic throwing and catching motions first. Then, when the players eventually start using gloves for catching, Monie has them begin in a position down on their knees because that forces them to put their hand up so they are holding the glove properly (facing up) for hard throws or hits near the face (see "Fielding From the Knees" in Coaches' Favorite Drills). By keeping the glove positioned properly, it is unlikely that the ball will hit them in the face when it comes to them.

☐ *Make a game out of anything you can.*

For working on speed running around the bases, **Monie Duran** likes to make a game out of the drills she runs.

> *"For running practice, I often set up a relay race around the bases or a quick race to a single base.*

**COACH
MONIE DURAN**

**San Dimas
Little League**
San Dimas, California

Although Monie Duran has coached kids from five to 12 years of age, she seems particularly devoted to some of the youngest ball players ... the T-ballers. To Monie, coaching is all about teaching the kids in a positive atmosphere and emphasizing teamwork, sportsmanship, and leadership. With T-ball, she feels the heaviest emphasis must be put on creating a fun atmosphere so that these young players will be motivated to come back for another season of learning.

We liked Coach Duran's description emphasizing fun with her youngest players through her flexibility during practices. Sometimes, if the situation calls for it, Monie may decide not to even play T-ball at practice. Especially when players are getting to know each other, she may instead have them play name tag to help them make friends with each other. We thank Monie for her contribution of drills for younger players. Look for them in Coaches' Favorite Drills.

When they're playing running games, the kids often don't realize that they're actually working their legs to increase speed and endurance."

Even setting up a "Simon Says" game to help players learn how to run quickly from base to base is fun and helpful. You can place a small group of players (maybe four) at home plate and tell them to listen to what "Simon Says" to do next. Then you can start shouting commands that resemble real play situations in a game such as, "Simon says run to first base and touch the base pad!" The kids should all run to first base and touch the base.

Then, after they all get to first base, you can say something like, "The ball is hit way up in the air and you run to second base." But, because you didn't say "Simon Says" they should stay on first base. You can explain to them that when the ball is hit up in the air, they need to wait to see if it is caught before they run to second base.

☐ *Set up practice groups based on ability.*

During practice, Coach Duran also tries to break the kids on her team into groups based on their abilities so each group can progress at a different level if it needs to. She likes to set up stations with a parent volunteer at each station. Then, regardless of the ability of the group, each group rotates through each station.

"At this age, baseball can be kind of boring for kids if there's a lot of waiting around, so we try to change activities as often as possible in a practice to keep them all occupied."

Monie tries not to have kids practice with each other. Instead she pairs small groups of players with an adult because most of them are really in need of one-on-one attention.

☐ *Release kids' extra energy so they pay better attention.*

Some of the hometown hero coaches believe in running kids during practice and others don't like to run kids. However, **Brig Sorber** uses running to help get younger kids to focus and pay better attention.

> *"Especially with younger kids, they're all excited when they first get to practice because they're seeing their friends in a different environment from school. So, the first thing I'll do is tell them to run a couple of hundred yards around the field and I always run with them. They get back and they're tired. But, now they're going to listen to you. Likewise, if during the practice I see things kind of falling apart, I'll pull everybody together and we'll run again. This really helps to get that extra energy out, especially with the younger players."*

Specific Fundamentals Work

Every good coach develops his or her own philosophies and special techniques for teaching players the fundamentals of baseball — hitting, throwing, fielding, pitching, catching, and so on. But, no matter how much of your own style you've developed, it's always valuable to hear how other coaches approach teaching fundamentals. Although you may not agree with each of these coaches on their philosophies for teaching certain skills, these tips offer some ideas to consider trying with your own team.

☐ *Find a catch phrase to remind a batter what to do at home plate.*

Steve Wagner knows that all players are different when it comes to developing hitting skills, and each one needs to be reminded of different things when they're up at bat. For example, one player might need a reminder to cock his bat, while another might need a reminder to get his weight back or bend his back leg. But Coach Wagner also knows that players tend to get nervous during games and don't always remember all the things that they have been taught about hitting in practice.

Coach Wagner uses a simple but effective method for giving his players reminders when they step up to home plate. Steve watches his players very carefully during practice and figures out a short catch phrase for each player that will remind him of some correction he needs to make whenever he hits. Then Steve uses this phrase as the player steps up to home plate.

> *"It's just catch phrases … for each player, it's a two- or three-word reminder that only he and the coach both understand, but that cues the player to remember what they have been taught in practice. Something you can quickly yell from the base coach's box like, 'down and back' or 'push it back' … those kinds of things."*

Coach Wagner says you can even have a little fun with the phrases you develop. Make up a funny saying just between you and the player that will remind him to correct the problem behavior.

☐ Don't teach too many mechanics to beginners, just encourage swinging.

A lot of coaches provide hitting instruction in the highly mechanical way you tend to see from the commercial videos available on the subject. But, **John Mangieri** thinks that young players learn better if a coach doesn't get so mechanical with hitting instruction.

> *"You can't put kids on an assembly line and teach them all the same thing. Kids are different shapes and sizes … some are short … some are tall … some have bigger middles than others … so you've gotta work with how they're going to swing instead of how some book says they ought to swing."*

For the younger ones, Coach Mangieri believes that you should go with anything that gives them confidence for the first few years. You can work on their mechanics when they are older. John gives his players a couple of basic tips on hitting and then he lets them take it from there, making it their own style of hitting as long as they're swinging at the ball. He even encourages young players to swing at bad pitches since that is better than just standing there looking at the ball every time it crosses the plate.

☐ *Hold a multi-station batting practice a couple of times each season.*

Russ Thompson recommends reserving a couple of your practices just for working on hitting. He recommends setting up a number of stations and rotating the players through each one a couple of times.

For one station, Russ pulls out the pitching machine and asks one player to load balls into it while the others at that station take turns hitting. Each player in the group takes a turn being the ball loader. At another station, Russ has a coach or a team pitcher throwing live pitches to a group of players. Coach Thompson sets up a third station with batting tees (the group at this station can rotate between batter, ball placer on the tee, and ball retrievers). A fourth station is set up with soft toss pitches.

At each station, the kids who aren't actively hitting or pitching can be ball retrievers. A parent volunteer or assistant coach can keep track of time and rotation order and yell, "Switch!" when it is time to go to another station. Setting up stations gives each player an opportunity to get 150 or more swings completed in a 90-minute practice.

☐ *Use pepper swings to analyze and correct bad hitting habits of older players.*

Coach **Richard Nagata** finds it easier to teach his older players the proper swinging techniques when they're not

COACH
RICHARD NAGATA

Aiea
Little League
Aiea, Hawaii

Richard Nagata is a big believer in removing any skills weaknesses or flaws in the older age youth players that he coaches to help them compete in the future. So, when players come to his team, Coach Nagata stresses fundamentals and encourages them to try playing positions that they may not have played for a few years so they can learn as much as possible about the game of baseball. He has seen several instances of players finding new favorite positions or surprising themselves at their skill in playing a position that they thought they couldn't play.

Coach Nagata also knows that players tend to worry more about their physical size and height as they get older. So, he always makes a point of letting all his players know that baseball skill doesn't always depend on size — even smaller players who haven't reached their full growth span yet can be good at baseball. Pep talks are an important part of Coach Nagata's philosophy.

swinging so hard, so he usually starts them out doing "pepper" swinging.

By setting up two pepper stations, with a batter and three or four fielders at each station, kids can stand about 30 feet from the batter, and about ten feet apart from each other. Then, by throwing hittable pitches, the batter can focus on hitting grounders to the fielders, trying to hit to each fielder in succession, moving from left to right. The purpose of this exercise is to focus on the mechanics of the batter, and to teach the batter to hit to different targets (each fielder in this case).

Coach Nagata stresses proper footwork, not striding too much or lunging at the pitch, and, if necessary, pivoting on the back foot to get a player's hip moving instead of locking the feet on the ground. He also makes sure that the hand location and shoulder angle are proper.

Using "pepper" swinging also allows Coach Nagata to teach his players how to move the ball all around to the right side or to pull the ball on the inside pitches, and so on.

"It's better to give a player 50 slow grounders than five hard ones."

Bill Sandry

Richard also coaches his players in smart batting such as making sure that the goal of two-strike hitting is making contact and not trying to kill the ball.

Once he has had a chance to correct critical deficiencies in each player's hitting mechanics, he allows the players to play pepper as a game. If the batter swings and misses a hittable pitch, he goes to the end of the line, and the player at the beginning of the line becomes the batter. Defensively, if any player misses a catchable grounder, he goes back to the end of the line. On the other hand, if any fielder catches a line drive or pop-up he automatically gets to be the next hitter.

☐ *Make bunting a required practice element until players have it mastered.*

Russ Thompson is a big fan of the bunt. In fact, he's such a fan that he requires every player on his team to bunt the first two pitches of a practice at-bat before they are allowed to swing away.

> *"I don't think there are enough kids these days who know how to bunt. Everyone wants to hit a home run. To encourage bunting, every kid on my team has to bunt the first two pitches, or however many it takes to lay down a successful bunt. They have to get a bunt down to first base and one down to third base, even if it takes them 30 pitches to do it, before they are allowed to hit."*

For younger players, Coach Thompson doesn't really teach bunting for base hits. Instead, he stresses sacrifice bunts, with the squaring stance and the goal of just getting the ball down to advance a runner. He tells them they have to really try to bunt the first pitch because if they don't, the third baseman is going to be living in their pocket for the next few pitches. So, that's why they have to practice bunting to get very good at it.

☐ *Make pitch counts COUNT, even during practice.*

Several hometown hero coaches are big believers in keeping pitch counts for youth players.

Coach **Dennis Dunn** recommends that even pitchers as old as 13 years throw a maximum of 75 pitches in a game. **JC Petersen** is also a big believer in pitch counts even though he knows that limiting your best pitchers by a pitch count during games can sometimes hurt the score. He likes to limit his pitchers' time on the mound during practice so that they can do their actual pitching during games. Therefore, JC usually does most of the pitching himself during practice for his team, even when he is coaching older players.

**COACH
DENNIS NICKERSON**

**Diamond Baseball
of Boulder**
Boulder, Colorado

Coach Nickerson sees his role in leading youth baseball as threefold: to teach kids baseball; to teach them about life; and to have fun. A veteran youth coach for over 18 years, we were impressed with Dennis' conviction for being up front with his players and their parents about following through with team rules. Dennis believes in being a man of his word and modeling that belief to his players at all times.

When we interviewed Dennis, we also sensed his true love of working with kids. His philosophy reflects how much he enjoys the mentoring aspect of coaching. To Dennis, youth baseball is mostly a tool to teach youngsters about life after baseball. The most important things they will take away from any season are the life lessons they'll put to use later on. Three cheers for Coach Nickerson's threefold approach to coaching!

For more information on pitch counts, see Dr. Lyle Micheli's comments in "Advice from the Experts" in Coaches' Tips & Advice.

☐ *Always pitch and catch to a spot … it's not just playing catch with the catcher.*

Although not all coaches teach pitching this way, **JC Petersen** emphasizes with his players to pitch to a spot instead of pitching to the plate.

> *"Always pitch and catch to a spot instead of pitching to the plate. But, I don't mean a tiny spot. We usually have the pitcher visualize something like a dinner plate in one of the four corners of the strike zone and pitch to that spot. Also, the catcher is always catching for a spot and not just sticking the mitt over the plate. You always hear coaches telling their players to just play catch with the catcher. But I figure if I have them aim for a spot that's about six inches wide, then they'll probably hit the spot that's two feet wide rather than just sort of aiming at the plate."*

☐ *Make pitching instruction simple with younger kids.*

Lloyd Rue breaks down his pitching instruction for his younger players (8- to 10-year-olds) into four simple steps: balance, stride, explosion (where the throw starts to come over the top and the stomach muscles are pulling down, chin forward), and finish (getting the right hip back through). For the "finish" step Coach Rue often gets his players to follow through by telling them to act like they are picking up a daisy or picking up a dandelion with their hand that has just released the pitch.

> *"Sometimes, I have the younger kids stand in a circle around a pitcher who's going through all the mechanics of a pitch, but without a ball in his hand.*

The other players watch him. Then, I ask them to make positive comments on what the pitcher did correctly. That's a real simple trick I use with players who are just beginning to pitch."

For more ideas on teaching pitching to young players, see "Word Association Pitching" in Coaches' Favorite Drills.

☐ *Stress balance and foot location for older players who must throw much further.*

With older players (11- to 13-year-olds) who have been pitching for awhile, **Richard Nagata** likes to make sure that the proper fundamentals are strong.

"With the older kids, because of the big change in distance (60 feet and 6 inches to the pitching rubber in many 13-year-old leagues), we like to make sure that they have strong fundamentals like balance and foot location. Balance is the key."

In fact, Coach Nagata has noticed that adjusting to the increase in distance when players move up to the next level is harder for the players who come up from a lower division as ace pitchers than it is for players who haven't pitched very much at all. A lot of times he sees these pitchers not using proper balance or body position, so he tries to stress those fundamentals.

Coach **Dennis Dunn** agrees with Coach Nagata on stressing proper mechanics and maintaining good balance. Coach Dunn recommends that coaches read books on pitching. He likes The Pitching Edge by Tom House because it goes into great detail about mechanics and training. (Tom House also has a series of videos that Coach Dunn likes.) Dennis also suggests checking out Dick Mills' "Pitching Success" newsletter and his website (www.pitching.com) for more information.

"Parents have to understand that it's not just the game. It's about friendship, sportsmanship, learning, developing, sacrificing, effort, having fun, setting and achieving goals, taking risks, learning to handle success and failure, and growing up."

Phil Swan

Coaching During Games

- [ ] Setting Lineups and Field Rotations
- [ ] Motivating and Encouraging Players
- [ ] Managing Parents and Assistant Coaches
- [ ] Working with Umpires

We can probably agree that winning is more fun than losing, all things being equal. Most coaches, even most parents, would likely agree with this statement when casually discussing the subject. In the heat of battle, however, even coaches and parents with the best of intentions can find their priorities being tested, and things can get ugly in a hurry.

For the most part, our hometown hero coaches believe that the key to good coaching during games is to keep the game in its proper perspective, encouraging kids to learn, exhibiting positive sportsmanship, and making "having fun" during games outweigh the importance of wins and losses. We agree with them. Many of the suggestions in this section are clearly designed to favor sportsmanship, fun, encouragement, and fairness.

As players get older, and their abilities and interest levels grow or wane, their individual priorities will change. By the time a child reaches the age of 13 or 14, he or she may quite naturally become more competitive about winning games. Until that time, we hope that the ideas in this section will help you to coach effectively and keep winning in its proper perspective for younger participants.

**COACH
DENNIS DUNN**

**Olney Boys &
Girls Club**
Olney, Maryland

We completely agree with Dennis Dunn's six "golden rules" of coaching expressed to us during his interview:

1. Give positive reinforcement to individuals and to the team in front of everyone.
2. Give individuals constructive criticism, on an as needed basis, and in front of no one.
3. Give the <u>team</u> constructive criticism with positive reinforcement.
4. Treat all players with respect, regardless of ability, to gain their confidence and make them want to play for you.
5. Teach sportsmanship first, winning second. Sportsmanship is treating coaches, teammates, opposing players, umpires and parents with the utmost respect.... and being a good winner and a good loser.
6. Teach respect for teammates and teamwork. Base your practices and games on the philosophy that great individuals do not win games, but teams do.

Setting Lineups and Field Rotations

Our hometown heroes gave us a variety of tips and advice on how they each set lineups and field rotations for games. However, our coaches were uniformly consistent on one point — the importance of emphasizing equity and fairness in whatever system is used. Here are their thoughts on making player assignments for games.

☐ *Prepare field assignments and batting order the night before the game.*

The key to preparing a good batting lineup and field rotation is a little time spent before you head to the field to play a game. Coach **Dennis Dunn** suggests preparing these things the night before a game. To help him organize his thoughts, he uses a lineup sheet that lists his team's players in one column and their fielding assignment by inning in rows across the top. This way he is sure to get a good rotation of players at various positions. During the season, he also prepares some quick notes about the previous game – what his team did right and what they struggled with. These notes come in handy for his pre-game talk with the players the next day.

Lloyd Rue also analyzes the results of his team's last game to help him prepare field assignments.

"It's best for the kids when I sit down and look at the results of the last game and think about where I need to place players for the next game, whatever my scheme or philosophy is. If I don't do that, then I tend to fall into a rut and have somebody playing in the same position all the time."

❑ *Survey players from two perspectives to match them with their best positions.*

Players can be surveyed from two perspectives — a player's preference for playing a certain position as well as his or her skill level in playing that position. **Dennis Dunn,** who coaches older youth players, uses both types of information to help him determine where to position players.

> *"At our first practice, I will ask the players to tell me their favorite positions. Then, in the first half of the season I will rotate players around to let them experience the different positions. I get a good feel for which players fit certain positions best and, as the season progresses, I will slowly move those players toward more time at that position. I try to give the less experienced players some time at second base and at third base where I know that they will get some (but not too much) action. As playoff time approaches, I will begin to position my stronger players in strategic positions. If I have a strong pitcher in with good speed I will be strong on the right side of the playing field. A good defensive first baseman is a must for all situations. As a general rule I will position my more experienced players in the middle field positions."*

❑ *Develop a system to rotate younger players fairly.*

"Baseball is a game of 'next-times' ... you always have another chance. If you blew that one, you'll get the next one."

Steve Wagner

Working on field rotations that are fair for younger players is important, especially when they haven't yet developed the skills or interest in playing a particular position. Every coach has his or her own system for rotating players. But, it's always interesting to see the systems that others use to promote a fair and equal rotation with younger kids.

Coach **Steve Wagner** has developed a system along with a couple of his coaching colleagues to ensure that every player plays at least four innings in every game. His system also rotates the team roster so that for every game during the season three players will end up playing all innings of that game. As Steve explains, the rotation works perfectly when your games last six innings and you have a team of 12 players who all show up for the game. But, it can also be modified for variations of those situations.

Essentially, Coach Wagner lays out a specific rotation for the first four games of a season. Then he just follows that series, repeating it throughout the season.

> "On my teams my kids usually have a great time because they all know they're going to play an equal amount of time from the best kid to the not-so-best kid. One of the first things I tell them is that I don't care how good they are or whether they're not any good at all … it doesn't matter. By the end of the season, they'll be good because they have each played a lot of baseball."

Here is a sample rotation like the one suggested by Steve.

Game 1

Number	Player	Inning 1	Inning 2	Inning 3	Inning 4	Inning 5	Inning 6
1	John	X	X			X	X
2	Tommy	X	X			X	X
3	Chad	X	X			X	X
4	Michael			X	X	X	X
5	Chris	X	X	X	X		
6	David			X	X	X	X
7	Brennon	X	X	X	X		
8	Curtis	X	X	X	X		
9	Corey			X	X	X	X
10	Justin	X	X	X	X	X	X
11	Ryan	X	X	X	X	X	X
12	Brian	X	X	X	X	X	X

Game 2

Number	Player	Inning 1	Inning 2	Inning 3	Inning 4	Inning 5	Inning 6
1	John			X	X	X	X
2	Tommy	X	X	X	X		

Number	Player	Inning 1	Inning 2	Inning 3	Inning 4	Inning 5	Inning 6
3	Chad			X	X	X	X
4	Michael	X	X	X	X		
5	Chris	X	X	X	X		
6	David			X	X	X	X
7	Brennon	X	X	X	X	X	X
8	Curtis	X	X	X	X	X	X
9	Corey	X	X	X	X	X	X
10	Justin	X	X			X	X
11	Ryan	X	X			X	X
12	Brian	X	X			X	X

Game 3

Number	Player	Inning 1	Inning 2	Inning 3	Inning 4	Inning 5	Inning 6
1	John	X	X	X	X		
2	Tommy	X	X	X	X		
3	Chad			X	X	X	X
4	Michael	X	X	X	X	X	X
5	Chris	X	X	X	X	X	X
6	David	X	X	X	X	X	X
7	Brennon	X	X			X	X
8	Curtis	X	X			X	X
9	Corey	X	X			X	X
10	Justin			X	X	X	X
11	Ryan	X	X	X	X		
12	Brian			X	X	X	X

Game 4

Number	Player	Inning 1	Inning 2	Inning 3	Inning 4	Inning 5	Inning 6
1	John	X	X	X	X	X	X
2	Tommy	X	X	X	X	X	X
3	Chad	X	X	X	X	X	X
4	Michael	X	X			X	X
5	Chris	X	X			X	X
6	David	X	X			X	X
7	Brennon			X	X	X	X
8	Curtis	X	X	X	X		
9	Corey			X	X	X	X
10	Justin	X	X	X	X		
11	Ryan	X	X	X	X		
12	Brian			X	X	X	X

COACH
TOM ALLEN

North East
Little League
North East, Maryland

Tom Allen has built his youth coaching career on his ability to sense unique characteristics and interests in his players, then to find ways to use those interests on the ball field. When we spoke with Tom, he told us about how he observes each player, watching their interactions with teammates and listening carefully to their needs. Then he uses what he knows about each player to encourage and motivate them to do their best. For example, Coach Allen has used a pitcher's intense interest in NASCAR racing to motivate him on the mound (see "Winning the Race" in Coaches' Memorable Stories.)

A soft-spoken man and a mechanic by trade, Tom is a classic example of a hometown hero, an ordinary person who devotes so much of his free time to teaching the youth of his community how to live and love the game. We commend his extraordinary efforts.

☐ Adjust rotations and playing times as kids get older.

Many of our coaches pay attention to the players' ages on the teams they coach. Keeping safety and skill level in mind, young players need to be rotated a lot to give them experience and confidence in playing several positions. Then gradually, as they get older, it becomes more appropriate to give some of the stronger players more time in the key field positions.

Each coach develops his or her own philosophy about when this transition should start, and there isn't always agreement about what age that happens. **Bob Karol** sees the transition beginning around ten years of age, at about fourth grade. **Tom Sutton** sees the transition starting a little earlier, around nine years old. For players who are eight and under, Coach **Lloyd Rue** always rotates them in different positions in the field and in the batting order.

But, all good coaches know that a variety of factors including age, coordination, confidence, safety, skills development, and individual team dynamics help to guide these decisions.

☐ Give players enough continuity in your rotation so that they can properly learn a position.

Tom Sutton makes a good point about being careful not to "over-rotate" players.

> *"You know, when I coach in T-ball and coach-pitch levels, I just rotate players around all the time. But as the kids get older, I find that it makes more sense to give them some continuity in the positions they play. If a player is constantly moving from third base to second base to shortstop to first base, he never learns any position very well because he's just not there long enough."*

Coach **Rob Cruz**, who coaches 10-year-olds, agrees with Tom about making sure that kids have the continuity they need to learn positions.

> *"I want to make sure that by the time my players finish their baseball season, they are better prepared to play baseball. So, I don't believe in playing kids everywhere just to play them. Pitching is a challenging situation in this regard. From time to time, if a kid who hasn't pitched before wants to pitch, then I'll give him that opportunity. But at the same time, I don't want a novice pitcher throwing 30 straight balls in a game and then I have to remove him. The other kids can't learn and get better if everyone is standing around watching players walk the bases."*

☐ *Keep safety in mind when positioning players.*

Ryan Callaham reminds us all that we should consider player safety as the top priority when thinking through a field rotation.

> *"I will not put a kid on a base when he's not ready for it just because his parents want that to happen. That's a good way to get a player hurt because it's not safe. For instance, putting a kid on first base who doesn't know how to catch a ball isn't a very smart move because he stands a very good chance of getting drilled in the head by a bad hop or a hard throw."*

☐ *Use "blowout" games to give players experience in new positions.*

In any sport it is inevitable that at some point during the season your team will get beaten, or that they will beat another team, by a large margin. In fact, sometimes your team finds itself in a "blowout" game situation where they are ahead or behind in runs to the point where there is very little chance of the game's outcome changing with further play. Coach **Bob Karol** points out that this is a great time to let some of the team's weaker players try an inning or two at an infield position, as long as you are conscious about their safety. It may even be appropriate to offer weaker players the chance to pitch to a few batters.

☐ *Make sure that parents know your playing time philosophy.*

Coach **JC Petersen** makes a good point about communicating your playing time philosophy to the team's parents. At the beginning of the season he tells the parents that he will try to play everybody for at least half of every game. But, he also reminds them that the length of youth baseball games can be unpredictable, and that sometimes a game with a very lopsided score will be called after only three-and-a-half or four innings have been played. Likewise, a game might be called off early due to inclement weather or playing time limits. As a coach, you may have planned for some players to get their infield time during the second half of a game and those innings never occur. This is a good reason to schedule weaker players in the early part of the rotation in some of the games.

☐ *With younger players, give all kids who ask a chance to pitch.*

Keeping safety in mind, **Bob Karol** believes that if a player expresses a desire to pitch a game, then go ahead and let him pitch. Are you going to put him on the mound in the last inning in a two to one game? No. But Coach Karol believes that you can certainly give that player an opportunity at any other time. Often times, players will surprise you and rise to the occasion. Even if it's just for one inning or less, that chance to pitch might be a player's only day in the sun.

☐ *With older players, establish a set pitching rotation early in the season.*

Dennis Dunn, who coaches older youth players, suggests establishing a pitching rotation that is set early in the season. Keeping in mind league rules regarding allowable pitching appearances or actual pitch counts, Dennis likes a three-player rotation, depending upon the strength of his pitchers. The starting pitcher (usually his best pitcher) goes three innings, the mid reliever goes two innings, and the closer goes the last two.

Coach Dunn wants his pitchers to become comfortable with their roles in the game. The starter knows how to prepare before game time. Mentally, he knows he will be facing the top of the lineup probably two times. He needs to be sharp. The mid reliever usually is the weakest of the three, a little slower than the starter but can get the ball over the plate. (This is where Coach Dunn often gives the less experienced kids who want to pitch during a game a chance to do so.) The mid reliever knows every game to start preparing himself mentally and physically to pitch in the third inning. Dennis' closing pitcher is usually his second best pitcher, but he must have good speed. Mentally the closer has the toughest job of all, especially in tight ball games.

☐ *Load strong hitters near the top of the batting order.*

As many of our coaches mentioned, **Ryan Callaham** generally tries to load the top of his lineup with strong batters.

> *"I generally want the first three or four batters to be good hitters. Maybe some of these kids don't run very fast, but they can really swat the ball. I do this because baseball is partly psychological, and if you can get a couple of players on base right away it tends to 'psyche up' the weaker hitters and gets them a little more willing to swing. For the rest of the lineup, I alternate one or two strong hitters, then a*

**COACH
RYAN CALLAHAM**

**Round Rock
Youth Baseball**
Round Rock, Texas

Like many of our hometown hero coaches, we had so many tips and drills from Ryan Callaham that we could have written most of a book on his thoughts alone. Ryan provided us with some great drills, like "Two Tee Batting" as well as lots of good tips on conducting practice, dealing with umpires and parents, and more.

Coach Callaham's main goal in coaching youth baseball is to build the desire in all his players to return for another season as well as to teach them all how similar the lessons of playing baseball are to the experiences of everyday life. Whether it's working together toward a common goal or learning to stay positive when they win as well as when they lose, Ryan Callaham's positive coaching style comes out in his contributions for this book. Thanks Ryan for some great advice!

weaker hitter, then a few more strong hitters, and so on. I try not to bunch up my weak hitters too much so we don't get three outs in a row."

Motivating and Encouraging Players

Keeping young baseball players focused and involved in a game can be a real challenge. We asked our hometown heroes what tricks they used to get (and keep!) their player's heads in the game. Our coaches use pre-game pep talks, they assign roles for players on the bench, and lots more. Here's what they told us.

☐ *Use a pre-game talk to focus and motivate players.*

Coach **Dennis Dunn** likes to prepare his team mentally as much as possible before a game. Each and every game he briefly reviews the responsibility of each position, from pitcher, to catcher, to first baseman, to outfield. He also covers the back-up responsibilities in game situations. He usually takes no more than ten minutes to do this. With younger players, Dennis believes that five minutes is sufficient.

Since he coaches older players, Coach Dunn also goes over the signs and when players should be stealing as well as reminders of other base running techniques.

"We also talk about the strengths and weaknesses of the other teams. A pre-game talk can be a very useful teaching tool."

☐ *Coach "mental attitude" all the time.*

The skill that Coach **Brig Sorber** works on the most isn't base running or throwing or hitting... it's mental attitude.

He believes that mental attitude is something you can coach with even the most physically challenged player.

> *"When they get to the plate, I just tell my players, 'That's YOUR plate buddy. The pitcher isn't doing you any favors. He's trying to strike you out.' I just try to get them mentally prepared and ready to focus on what they're doing. If you can get players really mentally focused and get their teammates behind them, cheering them on, it's just amazing what a challenged kid can do."*

☐ *Look for ways to involve players on the bench.*

One of the strategies that Coach **Rob Cruz** uses to keep his players focused is to give them responsibilities when they're on the bench. He has one player take care of the pitch count for the pitcher. He has another player keep track of the number of strikes and balls for his teammate in the batter's box. He has third player keep track of where hitters from the other team are hitting onto the field. Coach Cruz thinks that keeping his players involved in the game instead of sitting on the bench doing nothing really helps them stay focused and motivated to play hard.

☐ *Coach and advise with a positive spin.*

Bill Sandry believes in coaching and teaching throughout the whole game, constantly reassuring players or reemphasizing ready position or any little thing you can think of to try to keep them focused. He cautions that you shouldn't keep hitting the same player with the same reminders all night long, but you can emphasize major points like teamwork to everyone on the field.

> *"If a player makes the last out, he often feels like he's lost the game for the team and that's certainly not the case. I think when you teach teamwork you have to remind these kids of that. I personally try to teach teamwork throughout the whole game."*

HOMETOWN HERO PROFILE

COACH
BILL SANDRY

Bettendorf Barnstormer Baseball League
Davenport, Iowa

Bill Sandry's coaching philosophy is all about building skill, respect, integrity, and sportsmanship. Coach Sandry knows that teaching such life skills to his players is the best way he can make a lasting contribution to their growth and development.

To help him with this quest, Bill enlists the help of the players on other teams in his league for peer mentoring. Coach Sandry asks older kids to attend practices with younger players, explaining fundamentals and practicing right along side them in a simulated game. The "kids teaching kids" approach is a good learning experience for both groups of players.

Bill Sandry's enthusiasm exudes his love of the game. From the smell of grass on an old, worn out baseball to the thrill of watching his players collect autographs at the College World Series, Bill is clearly out to pass his love of the game on to the next generation.

Coach **Brig Sorber** agrees.

> *"You just have to encourage these kids all the time, especially at the younger ages and when they strike out. Just let them know that if they go down swinging, that's all you're looking for."*

Often times, Coach Sorber will encourage a player after striking out by saying something like, "You know, that's the best swing you've had this game!" or "That's the best swing you've had this week." If there's something positive you can think up to say, it really helps to build kids' confidence.

Coach **Rod Hudson** reminds all coaches that keeping a positive demeanor is for the parents as well as the players. As a team coach, you are always "on display," which means that you are committed to practice positive coaching for everyone involved in the game.

Coach Hudson uses lots of encouraging comments like, "Great throw," or "Nice catch," to his players while they are on the field.

☐ *Look for unique, positive traits to emphasize in each player.*

Coach **Brig Sorber** makes sure that his positive coaching emphasis reaches every player on his team. He thinks it's important that a coach observe each player individually and pick out one thing that sticks out as a real positive trait with that player. He even turns a player's size into a positive comment if he needs to.

> *"We've had a couple of guys on our team who were bigger, kids that were slower, or they weren't as aggressive. Maybe they weren't really very athletic either. But, you can still encourage them to play their best by comments like, 'Listen, you're one of the biggest kids on the team. Look at the shoulders on you. We've gotta get you swinging this bat*

because you're a one-man wrecking crew. All we have to do is get your bat out there.'

Or, for another player who is small, before he gets up to bat, you can say, 'You know what? You're the fastest kid on this team. We've gotta have you on base. So, do everything that you can to get there because we can use your speed.'

When a player knows they have something to give, they're willing to give more. If they look at themselves as an asset to the team instead of a burden, they will play better."

☐ *Keep players "up" in tough situations.*

When games or seasons get tough and the players start getting down, Coach **Jay Hinson** switches his coaching strategy to an "inning" philosophy. Instead of working to win an entire game, he tells his players to concentrate on having great innings, one inning at a time. That seems to make a game less overwhelming for them than to think about doing well for a whole game. Coach Hinson used this philosophy one season where his team's game record half way through the season was at three wins and six losses. He switched his coaching strategy, encouraging his players to "win" innings, and his team ended up winning the last six games of that season.

☐ *Use teaching moments wisely.*

Some of our coaches caution against too much teaching during a game. Coach **Jon Brainard** believes that you shouldn't "conduct practice" during a game, constantly interrupting the flow of the plays. Instead, the time to correct or strengthen skills is during the next practice. Jon does understand that there are some situations where you can and should teach a player during the action of a game. But, if you want to use the situation for teaching, then Jon recommends speaking with the player privately after he or she has returned to the bench.

COACH JAY HINSON

Cheraw Dixie Youth Baseball
Cheraw, South Carolina

In the 25 years that Jay Hinson has been coaching baseball, he has learned exactly how to motivate his players to keep trying during a game. We thought his "inning" philosophy was a great way to focus players on the task at hand and not get overwhelmed by thinking too far ahead. Coach Hinson told us that he asks his players to think about playing baseball by winning one inning at a time, not by winning a game at a time. For kids, that's a much more reasonable length of time to ask them to concentrate on playing baseball. Then, with more and more innings completed, Coach Hinson finds his players focusing a lot more on their small accomplishments and not so much on the overall score.

We really enjoyed Jay's stories, some of which you'll see in Coaches' Memorable Stories. It's great to see such long-term dedication to coaching kids.

Managing Parents and Assistant Coaches

When coaches volunteer to lead youth baseball teams, they inherently know that they are volunteering to manage a group of kids. But few first-time coaches realize that their commitment must often extend far beyond their players. The team's parents, whether they serve as assistants on the field or just cheer from the sidelines must also be managed to ensure a successful season for all. Many of our hometown hero coaches have developed strategies for managing the "non-youth" portion of the team, tapping into their available skills and focusing their energy in positive ways. Here are some ideas worthy of consideration.

☐ *Give parents a job to do during the games.*

One of the best ways to get parents positively involved in the games is to give them a specific job to do. Coach **JC Petersen** uses parents on or around the bench. He asks one parent to keep track of the lineup and make sure that players are getting ready when it is close to their turn to hit. He assigns another parent to monitor the "on deck" area, making sure that players are careful not to hit each other during practice swings.

Monie Duran also uses parents to assist during games.

> *"I like to get my parents involved because, otherwise, I've found that a coach becomes somewhat of a baby sitter, especially with the younger kids. I try to get parents involved by scheduling a game for each of them to bring snacks for the team. I also assign them dugout duty, helping with a variety of tasks like keeping the lineup going, making sure that the players are sitting in the order in which they're batting, keeping the kids focused, helping the team to cheer on teammates, and helping players in and out of their gloves and hats when it's time to go back out on the field."*

☐ *Set expectations up front for appropriate parental behavior at games.*

John Mangieri, who works in sales when he's not coaching, deals with parents like he deals with his customers, by setting expectations for appropriate behavior at games right up front with them. He speaks with them about his rule for no eating or drinking in the dugout. He also lets them know that he alone decides where to position players and how the lineup will work. During the games, the coach is in charge of the players and their actions.

Coach **Jeff Mathis** follows a similar strategy. He lets his parents know up front that the coach will make the decisions during games. When he has parents who get out of hand and start to criticize his coaching decisions, Jeff will usually offer them his hat and clipboard. He has yet to get a taker for his job.

☐ *Position parent coaching assistants according to their strengths.*

Parents will come to your team with a wide variety of skills and talents. Some will be very knowledgeable about youth baseball while others will be quite naive … and some will think they know a lot more about the sport than they really do. Coach **Bill Sandry** always tries to use parents where they are most effective.

> *"If the team has somebody who really likes teaching baseball, you ought <u>not</u> to have them coach third base. Instead, have somebody else coach third base, and put your "teacher" in the dugout so he or she can teach the kids all through the game. My passion is teaching the kids the game. I've got another dad who loves being in control, so third base coach is a good spot for him because he can call lots of plays."*

COACH JEFF MATHIS

DeMotte
Little League
DeMotte, Indiana

This hometown hero has only one coaching philosophy … "make sure that everybody has fun and learns" … an impressive statement to be sure. But, what impressed us was Jeff's explanation of "everybody." He maintains that coaches need to be having as much fun as the players. Jeff knows that players who see their coach enjoying the time spent on the field are motivated to play hard for him and enjoy the whole experience a lot more.

Jeff gains respect and trust from his players by showing his willingness to do anything that he asks them to do. For example, if he asks his team to run a lap for warm-ups, Jeff will run it with them. If a player is struggling with a skill, Jeff will get out on the field and play with him … whatever it takes to make that player realize that he can do it. Thanks for your dedication, Coach Mathis.

❑ *Use parent base coaches during team practices as well as games.*

Coach **Bill Sandry** likes to end all of his practices with base running skills so his base coaches can practice sending, holding, giving signals while his players respond. Coach Sandry tries to put players in different situations with the base coaches in position. That way, the players get their conditioning practice as well as experience communicating with the base coaches all at once.

Working with Umpires

When it comes to mentoring appropriate ways to interact with baseball umpires, everybody — the players, the parents, members of the other team, even the umpires themselves — will look to the coach to set the standard. Our hometown hero coaches were unanimous on this issue, all of them believing that it is critical for the coach to lead the way in serving as a positive role model for his or her team. Here are some specific thoughts.

❑ *Model behavior that teaches players to treat umpires with respect.*

Coach **Steve Wagner** understands that umpires are just out there trying to do their best at their job, making good calls and making sure that everyone plays fair. Steve should know because he often umpires games for his league. Steve knows that coaches who show respectful behavior when dealing with umpires get listened to a lot more than those who come out yelling.

> *"As an umpire, if a coach comes out screaming and hollering at me, I'm much less inclined to listen to him much. I'll be nice ... then I'll politely tell him to go back into the dugout because I couldn't understand a word he is yelling. On the other hand,*

if a coach calls time out and they're nice and they want to talk to me about something that they have a valid concern over, then, by all means, I'll listen to what they have to say."

Coach **John Mangieri** agrees. He realizes that a lot of umpires at the youth level don't have a whole lot of experience and can tend to get beaten up verbally by overly aggressive parents or coaches. As the role model for the players, the coach can set the tone for positive interactions with the umpire right from the beginning.

☐ *Learn the rule book well so your questions are legitimate.*

Coach **Steve Wagner** also recommends that all coaches learn the rule book as well as they can. If a coach knows the rules well, then they know when they have a problem and when they don't. Rules vary from league to league, and from age division to age division, particularly with pitching and base running. It's important that coaches familiarize themselves with rules and rule modifications.

☐ *Remind players and parents that everyone, even an umpire, makes mistakes.*

One of the biggest things that coaches and players tend to forget is that the umpires at the youth level are often learning just like the kids are. Coach **Bill Sandry** realizes that the league is in the business of training umpires as well as training kids. Just like the kids, if an umpire is always getting yelled at, he or she is not going to want to call very many games or come back to umpire in future seasons.

Coach Sandry tries to teach his players respect for umpires by reminding his players that nobody is perfect, that mistakes will be made, but that those mistakes will rarely cost a team the entire game.

"I see a lot of coaches that are ripping into umpires for a questionable call and pretty soon it's the umpire's fault that they lost the game. Then, I hear the kids talking amongst themselves afterwards and they don't talk about that missed cutoff in the second inning or the other mistakes the team players made … the things that really cost them the game. Instead they'll talk about that one play where the umpire made a questionable call."

Coach **Russ Thompson** has a similar philosophy regarding umpires. He tells his players that over the course of a season the umpires are going to make a lot less mistakes than those made by the coaches and the players. Of course, Coach Thompson has disagreements with umpires and he'll speak with an umpire over an interpretation of a rule. But, he tries not to question judgment calls because it just sets a bad example for his players. And if the coach starts it, then the kids follow the coach's lead. If the coaches and the kids are yelling about something, then the parents get into it. Pretty soon you've got 25–30 people all on the umpire's back, and that isn't fair to the umpire or the integrity of the game.

☐ *Share your comments with the umpire privately and between innings or after the game.*

Many of our coaches suggest that it is best to hold your comments until you can approach the umpire privately and between moments of game-time action.

Coach **Jeff Mathis** likes to hold his comments for the umpire until after the game is over and the other coaches have left the field. He does make it a point to express his disagreement with a call because that can often be a learning experience for both the coach and the umpire. But, he tries never to interrupt the umpire during a game. Coach **Bill Sandry** also believes that a coach shouldn't ever try to show up an umpire or point out an obvious mistake in the middle of play.

The philosophy that Coach **Tom Sutton** carries to his players is to remind them that the umpire is not there with "an agenda." Rather, he or she is just there to call the game in the best and fairest way possible. To show his players that he respects the umpire, Coach Sutton also holds his questions until the time between innings or after the game so he can ask the umpire about a call in a polite and unthreatening manner.

For more good information on working with umpires, see the summarized comments from our interview with Rich Nedimyer, a certified umpire, in "Advice from the Experts" in Coaches' Tips & Advice.

**COACH
TOM SUTTON**

**Germantown
Athletic Club**
Germantown, Maryland

Good "teamsmanship" is a big priority with the teams that Tom Sutton coaches. He believes in working with his players on interacting with one another in a positive way and learning how to work together towards one goal. Everybody on Coach Sutton's team understands that he or she has a role to play ... not everybody can be a pitcher or a first baseman ... but respect for each other and doing your part for the good of the team goes a long way with this hometown hero.

When we spoke with Tom, he spoke about good sportsmanship in general. Like many of our hometown heroes, Tom promotes players giving positive feedback to each other ... comments like, "Good throw!' or "Nice hit!" But, we also liked the fact that he encourages his players to compliment the players on the opposing team when they make a good hit or play. Good show, Coach Sutton!

*"If I can finish
coaching a game and
see 13 kids smiling,
then we won ... in
my mind, we won."*

Jeff Mathis

Making It Fun

☐ Making Practice Fun
☐ Organizing Special Events
☐ Motivating and Encouraging Creatively

COACH
RUSS THOMPSON

**Keene Cal Ripken
Baseball Association**
Keene, New Hampshire

Russ Thompson has been coaching for nine years, a long time. But, he admits that the first season or two was a challenge for him, even though his years of playing baseball in high school and all through college had him knowing the sport like the back of his hand. (See his story, "Split Decision" in Coaches' Memorable Stories.)

Russ learned to coach by watching the actions of other coaches in his league. He gathered that collective coaching wisdom from others to create his own unique coaching style, based on the constant that no matter what level of players he coaches, they're all really looking to have fun. Coach Thompson knows that as kids get older, they often look for more competition, but they still want it to be fun. So, a good coach has to provide the right balance for his players. Our conversation with Coach Thompson proved that he's found that balance.

In the end, it all comes down to creating a positive experience for the players on your team. To a coach, that means providing a good learning experience and being able to inspire and motivate your players to do their best. To kids, it primarily means having fun. This collection of tips and advice offers some good "word of mouth" ideas for making youth baseball a wonderful and memorable experience.

Making Practice Fun

Kids will work hard for you if you mix a little fun into their practice routines. Here are some great ideas from our hometown hero coaches for incorporating fun into practices.

☐ *Turn a drill into a contest at the end of each practice.*

Coach **Russ Thompson** likes to have a contest at the end of every practice to give the kids something to look forward to. He also likes to end practice on a positive note.

"If we've got the pitching machine set up in the outfield, then we'll have a fly ball contest to see who can catch ten in a row. I've also done a bunting contest where I'll draw a box along the third baseline and one along the first baseline, then every kid gets ten pitches to try and bunt it into the box. Another good one is a ground ball fielding contest."

Coach Thompson usually makes the prize something simple like a bottle of a sports drink or a candy bar. He likes the contest idea because the kids are learning and practicing but they're doing it in a fun way.

☐ Play name games at practice to help younger kids bond as a team.

Sometimes it makes sense to play a "non-baseball" game at baseball practice, especially to help younger kids to learn each others' names. Coach **Monie Duran**, who coaches younger players, likes to use games of tag to help her players learn names.

"I like to have fun with the kids, so sometimes we may not even play baseball at practice. Especially when they are getting to know each other, we may play name tag, basically a tag game with one person being the 'tagger' or 'it' who tries to tag any other player on the team. The special catch to this tag game, however, is that the 'tagger' cannot tag anyone else and pass the tag along unless he or she can also say that player's first name correctly."

☐ Invite a high school coach or high school players to assist with a practice.

One of our hometown hero coaches, **JC Petersen**, suggests inviting the area varsity baseball coach or a couple of varsity players to come to a team practice. He doesn't ask them to stay for long or even to run the practice. He just likes them to talk to the kids for a few minutes or to run a couple of plays with the kids in the field.

> *"One time, I had a left-handed pitcher from the local high school varsity team come to a practice. He talked to the kids a bit about pitching and stealing bases ... they were in awe of this 'real' high school baseball player ... then he went onto the mound for about 15 minutes and picked the kids off at first base. The kids loved it, and I think the 17-year-old got just as much of a thrill out of it! There are a lot of people out there who are more than happy to help if you ask them."*

☐ *Hold a series of special staggered short practices to focus on small groups of players.*

Mixing up a practice format is always fun for kids. If you are looking for a way to give some extra attention to each individual, hold a special batting practice where the players arrive at pre-designated and staggered 30-minute intervals over a two-hour window. For each 30-minute span, you only schedule two to three players to be on the field with the coach. Then you choose one skill to work on in your small group — hitting, fielding, base stealing, catching fly balls, and so on.

For example, for a team with 12 players, have three kids come to the field from 5:30 to 6:00 p.m., then the next three from 6:00 to 6:30, the next three from 6:30 to 7:00, and the last three from 7:00 to 7:30 p.m. Of course, you have to schedule this in advance (by phone or sign-up sheet at a previous game) and remind the players how important it is to get there on time so they have their full 30 minutes of instruction. But, for many kids, getting 30 minutes of focused attention is just as valuable as working for two hours with a large group.

**COACH
JC PETERSEN**

**Okemos Baseball/
Softball Club**
Okemos, Michigan

JC Petersen told us that he just plain loves baseball — no other sport compares. So, he really emphasizes the fun part of the game for his teams. During practices, Coach Petersen stays away from long group lectures on rules or school-like handouts. Instead, he likes to get his players, even the youngest ones, right out on the field and start them playing in a safe way, teaching them the rules as they go along.

To keep things interesting, Coach Petersen likes to bring in new mentors for his team. He has been known to ask the varsity baseball coach from the local high school and some of the varsity players to come to a practice. Even 15 minutes of working with the kids provides them with enough excitement to last the rest of the practice ... and in Coach Petersen's experience, the varsity coaches and players get as much enjoyment out of their experience as the kids. We applaud Coach Petersen's creative coaching efforts!

Organizing Special Events

To youth sports players, getting together with friends for a good time is often just as important, if not more so, than participating in organized practices and games. Kids like the inclusive feeling of team membership, and being involved in special team events can serve as a valuable bonding experience for them. Try a few of these great ideas for promoting teamsmanship ... and just plain having fun together!

☐ *Organize a mid-season pizza or ice cream party.*

Coach **Monie Duran** organizes get-togethers and parties for her players, especially in the first half of a season. She uses these casual situations as ice breakers for her kids so everyone can learn each others' names and become friends. Making friends also helps the kids to begin to build trust with each other.

> *"It also helps the parents get to know each other. This helps when our team is responsible for contributing time to some of the league jobs like working the snack bar. It makes us have a good time while we're working because we know each other and we have fun with it."*

☐ *Take your players to a high school or college-level game.*

In almost every town, there are inexpensive baseball events that you can attend with your team and a few of their parents. Sometimes, you can even find a special baseball event to attend with your players. In a recent season, Coach **Bill Sandry** even had a chance to take his players to the College World Series that was being played in a city close by. Some of the kids were able to get autographs of a few players and they had a really good time.

❑ *Arrange for your team to be the "run-on" team for a high school or college game.*

Many high school, college, or minor league ball clubs will allow youth teams to "run on" to the field with the players during the pre-game announcements. There is nothing more exciting to a young ball player than being able to jog out to a base or outfield with a "real baseball player" as the starting positions are called out over the loudspeaker. Check with your local schools and minor league teams to see if this opportunity exists in your hometown.

❑ *Plan a moms' or dads' coaching day for a game during the season.*

Coach **John Mangieri** tried a moms' coaching day one season where all of the moms of children on the team had to perform all the coaching duties during a baseball game. The regular coaches and any other dads had to sit on the sidelines and were not allowed to help coach in any way, just to cheer for the team players. If done with a lighthearted spirit by all, this can be a fun activity.

> *"Everybody had a great time watching the moms chalk the fields, set the lineups, keep the score book, run the players in and out for changes, and so on. The kids even got a kick out of it and had to help their moms out with details a lot."*

An all dads' coaching day is also fun, again with the regular coaches sitting on the sidelines.

❑ *Plan a "parents/kids" game during the season.*

During the season, find time to have a game between the kids and the parents. A parents/kids game is always a blast for everyone involved in the game. Prior to the game:

- "Advertise the Prize" - If the kids win (and they should, by the way), the parents could treat them to ice cream. If the parents win, the kids might be asked to give their parents back rubs when they get home (they'll probably need it).

- Meet with the parents. Encourage them to exercise restraint. There are always one or two parents who are very competitive by nature, and have difficulty "holding back." Remind them that having fun and building the kids' confidence is more important than winning the game. Try to find ways for the kids to succeed like making an occasional overthrow or striking out on purpose. Find a way to put the kids in a position to win without "giving" them the game.

- Review the rules. Depending on the ages/abilities of your players, have the parents hit with one hand or with an opposite batting stance (that is, "righties" become "lefties"), or have the parents (except pitcher and first baseman) field and throw with their opposite hands … anything to make it a fair game.

☐ Invite another league's team for a scrimmage and pizza party.

Coach **John Mangieri** likes to invite a team from another youth league in a neighboring county to join his team for an afternoon of scrimmaging and pizza. He selects a team with a similar age grouping and skill level if possible.

☐ Declare one regular game in the season as your "mess-around" game.

This is a game in which you let players play whatever they want. You let the kid who's wanted to catch all year play catcher and the kids who have wanted to pitch all year pitch. That's called a "mess-around" game, an idea passed on by Coach **Steve Wagner**, who asks his players to let him know where they want to play so he can give them an opportunity to do so during this game. Coach Wagner knows that giving a player a chance at a new position in a real game situation can pay off for that player as well as the team.

> *"The 'mess-around' game is how my son got started playing catcher. I've also found four pitchers that way over the years and all kinds of position players. If a player wants to try something, let that player try it."*

For more information, refer to the "Mess-Around Game" Drill in Coaches' Favorite Drills.

☐ *Get your team together on a weekend or summer day for some baseball fun.*

Now THIS is dedication to kids! Coach **John Mangieri** conducts a week-long half-day summer camp at his house for kids who play on his teams. His players arrive at his house at 8:00 a.m. to the smell of French toast, waffles, eggs, or pancakes being prepared by the coach! Then he plans a variety of activities for the kids — a special guest speaker like someone's grandfather to talk about how youth baseball used to be 50 years ago or a lesson in reading major league standings in the newspaper — all things surrounding the sport of baseball.

> *"In the late morning, I take the kids outside to a ball field for about 90 minutes of drills and scrimmaging, finishing by playing a workup game (see 'Workup Game' in Coaches' Favorite Drills.) Then we all go back to my house for a quick dip in the pool before the kids' parents pick them up at noon. I charge $25 for the entire week and all the proceeds go into the team kitty."*

On Friday, the last day of camp, Coach Mangieri holds a sports triathlon where the kids have to ride a bike a mile, run a mile, and then swim four laps in his pool. What a conditioning routine!

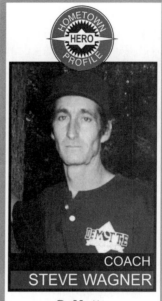

COACH
STEVE WAGNER

DeMotte
Little League
DeMotte, Indiana

Coach Wagner believes that repetition and positive reinforcement builds baseball players. That means everyone on Steve's teams gets equal playing time, the strong players as well as the weak ones. To ensure such equity, Steve puts a lot of time into his player rotations at the beginning of each season. In fact, he shared with us his formula for rotating players so that each one gets to play a minimum of four innings in every six inning game. (See "Setting Lineups and Field Rotations" in Coaches' Tips & Advice.)

Coach Wagner also believes that maintaining an encouraging attitude with your players will net much bigger gains in skills and make a memorable experience for all team members. Steve reminded us all that baseball is a game of "next times" — you always have another chance to get the next one — that's a great philosophy to carry in your back pocket.

❑ *Plan an end-of-season party with special mock awards.*

Coach **Rod Hudson** always holds an end-of-season party at a local pizza restaurant. He invites all the players, of course, as well as any parents and siblings who want to join in the fun. At the restaurant, Rod makes sure that the team members get their own special table, then he serves up pizza and sodas for all.

But, the real treat comes after the eating is over. Rod highlights the accomplishments of each player, telling the crowd about all the great ways that each team member has grown during the season. Of course, he uses some basic statistics, like who had the best on-base percentage, and so on. But, Coach Hudson also takes time to think up a mock Baseball Recognition Award for each player, sometimes related to a character trait and not to a baseball skill. Then he presents each player with a certificate naming that mock award.

A fun twist he sometimes adds to his awards is to link each of his team players to a professional player, noting their similarities in character or skill. For example, a player who shows great leadership on the ball field might receive the "Paul Molitor Award" for showing great sportsmanship, teamwork, and pride during the season.

End-of-season parties can be held at any location, even on the ball field after the last game, and they provide a nice wrap-up for the team's achievements.

Motivating and Encouraging Creatively

Some very creative brains were at work when these ideas were passed to us! We can almost guarantee that you'll find at least one new strategy to try with your team.

❏ *Distribute treats to younger players for a job well done.*

Kids love treats of any kind. Just notice their reaction to goodie bags they get at parties — they treasure getting little prizes and sweets. This tactic can be used to reward younger kids during games. Especially for 5- to 8-year-olds, buy a large bag of mixed candy or some small prizes, and have a parent hold it during the game. Then, if a player makes a nice catch, give them a couple of treats. If a player does the right mechanical things, but makes an error, give them a few treats for doing the right things (that is, moving his feet well, keeping his glove down, charging the ball, and so on.) Focus on whether the player tried to do the right things, not just making the actual hit or catch. You can also give treats for positive attitudes or for good hustle.

❏ *Wear rally caps to fire up your team.*

You can do fun things like using rally caps to encourage any and all kinds of positive teamsmanship. For example, if your team is behind by six runs in the bottom of the fifth inning, fire them up by turning your cap inside out and encouraging them to do the same. Rally caps have been used for years at all levels and they're still a fun source of inspiration for the kids.

❏ *Reward excellent plays during a game with a team "cap slap."*

Coach **Rod Hudson** uses the "cap slap" as a way to recognize an excellent play by a team member. During a game, if a player makes a spectacular catch, executes a brilliant double play, hits a grand slam, or shows some other great skill, that player can look forward to a "cap slap" by all his teammates at the end of the inning. A perfectly executed "cap slap" occurs when the entire team, plus the coaches, surround a player as he comes off the field, all take off their baseball caps, and use them to simultaneously slap the honored player on his head a couple of times.

"Baseball is a game of chances and opportunities ... preparation plus confidence plus opportunity to perform = success and fun."

Rod Hudson

The coach announces a cap slap by raising his own cap up over the honored player's head and saying something like, "This is for that fabulous catch, Robbie, out in left field." The kids love to join in this quick and fun way to congratulate their teammate. A "cap slap" also binds the team together and motivates them, just like a mid-game chant or cheer.

☐ Select a special team captain for each game played.

Special recognition can come in various forms, even if it's being designated as the official "team leader" for a game. You can select a different captain for each game and have that player lead a cheer before the game starts. You can also have that player go out for the umpire's meeting if the umpire will allow it — anything that will give that player the spotlight as often as possible. Many coaches also make it part of the team captain's duties to offer encouragement to his or her other teammates and to coax other team players to do the same. For example, if a player strikes out, the team captain can make sure that teammates slap that player's hand and tell him to "get it next time."

☐ Award "game balls" or "team pins" after games.

At the conclusion of every game, a lot of coaches award a game ball to one or two of the team's players for a job well done, and this is an effective (and fairly inexpensive) way to encourage and reward players. You should be able to find baseballs for about $2.00 each at any sporting goods store. When awarding game balls, you should try to focus on effort and attitude more than just physical performance. Write "Game Ball" and the date on the ball in permanent ink. At the conclusion of each game, during your post-game talk with the kids, give a game ball (or two) and explain the reasons you chose that particular recipient. Try to make sure that everyone on the team receives a game ball by the end of the season. The kids will keep track of who has been awarded this honor and it is very important not to forget any of the players.

Hometown hero Coach **Rod Hudson** uses an interesting variation for his team awards. He purchases inexpensive hat or lapel pins sporting some sort of baseball design and awards his players a pin for good sportsmanship, a great play, showing leadership, and so on. The players can wear these pins on their caps during the season as badges of honor. Again, Coach Hudson makes an effort to get a pin to every player on his team during the season. He gives out two or three pins at the conclusion of each game. He also likes to split his awards between "game" awards (for great physical or mental plays) and "team" awards (for showing leadership and team spirit).

☐ *Show team sportsmanship by giving the other team a game ball or candy bars.*

Here is an idea that really models good sportsmanship to your players as well as the players on the opposing team. Coach **John Mangieri** occasionally has his team present the opposing team with a game ball for a job well done. Sometimes, he also brings candy bars or other treats to distribute to the other team. What a great way to show everyone on the ball field what true sportsmanship is like.

☐ *Submit game summaries in the local newspaper to highlight your team.*

Think of how exciting it is for a 9-year-old to see his or her name printed in the newspaper! Many communities allow youth team coaches to submit written game summaries to the local papers and this is a great way to make the season fun for everyone. Keep in mind that when you prepare a game summary, you should try not to focus only on winning pitchers and home run hitters. Instead, try to focus equally on good fielding plays, on-base percentages, great

HOMETOWN HERO PROFILE

COACH JOHN MANGIERI

Bettendorf Barnstormer Baseball League
Davenport, Iowa

As far as Coach Mangieri is concerned, youth baseball is all about development. John believes in giving the kids a really good foundation in how to go about playing the game by teaching them fundamental skills. Then, as the season progresses he builds some success with his players and they have fun so that they want to come back next year.

Before we interviewed John, we had heard about his famous "Camp Mangieri," his homegrown version of summer baseball camp for his players. At the week long Camp Mangieri, every morning starts off with the coach cooking breakfast for the team. Then it's off for a fun day of practicing baseball skills, swimming, and general summertime fun. These kids even learn how to read major league standings in the local newspaper. You can bet Coach Mangieri's team is a popular one to be placed on in this league!

hustle, and so on, remembering to give equal credit to all players throughout the season.

☐ *Send your team members and their parents a post-game email summary.*

Coach **Rod Hudson** is a master at post-game emails. He makes special note during his team's games of something that each player does well, even if it is working hard on improving his or her playing skills. Then he turns his memories into great game summaries that are fun for all to read. Here is a great example of his handy work with his "Twins" youth baseball team:

> *"Twins Baseball Recap: our players continue to improve with smart team play and showing a lot of heart and desire in our play. We came back on the Phillies in Friday's game after being down several runs. Miscues are being minimized, which are part of development. Our players are working hard and enjoying themselves, finding successes and having some FUN!*

> *"Team-wise, we perfectly executed three "pickles" or pick-off rundowns over the weekend. Our throws from catchers to the bases are becoming more authoritative. Our shortstops and second basemen are covering on balls hit to the outfield. Our guys are learning how to play multiple defensive positions. We are hitting the ball well, getting on base, and getting key RBIs. In the game versus the Cubs our pitchers combined to allow only one hit and one run.*

> *Now for the 'A to Z' ... 'Gentleman' Josh continues to captain the middle of our defense, Twins Game Award for his Leadership. James pitched two solid innings and is seeing the ball better at the plate. Nick made a great catch in right, still learning baseball stuff, healthy swing, starting to make contact, Twins Game Award for the catch. 'Rockin' Robbie is becoming one of the most improved players in league, great clutch hit ... Jason is one of our role*

models for hustle and desire, reliable wherever he plays, pitched four shutout innings, key hits. Ryan anchors our first base with his leadership and hustle … he'll eventually get his power groove at the plate. Easton is having fun with his hustle and confident play, key hit. Mike demonstrated his confidence and ability on the great catch in right, Twins Game Award for great catch. Our catcher, Alex, is hitting for power … GO TWINS!!!

Note the nicknames that Coach Hudson uses in his emails. Rod has been doing this for years as it endears players and coaches alike. His players have held nicknames such as "clutch," "hollywood," "mad dog," and so on, anything that might be tied to that player's demonstrated baseball skill, his real name, or his personality. Here are some additional examples: "Cool" for the player who is never bothered by anything, "Sweet Swing" for the player who has a great swing and follow through, "Crazy legs" for the player who is the fastest runner, "Big Hurt" for the power hitter, and so on. Coach Hudson develops his names throughout the season as he observes his players. Then he'll use them during the games as he coaches the team and as an endearing motivator to his players.

Coach Hudson makes it a point NEVER to use nicknames that are offensive in any way: no reference to player size, weight, race, and so on. Kids want a nickname of which they can be proud.

"If you put having fun and respecting your teammates ahead of everything else, the winning and losing takes care of itself."

Tom Sutton

Advice from the Experts

☐ Dr. Lyle Micheli -- Minimizing Sports Injuries
☐ Rich Nedimyer -- An Umpire's Perspective
☐ Bob Bigelow -- Adapting a Coaching Style for Children

In addition to our valuable tips and advice from our hometown heroes, we thought it worthwhile to provide expert opinions on three additional and important topics.

Every coach wants to make sure that he or she is leading players through activities in a safe and effective manner. We contacted Lyle Micheli, M.D., an authority and author on preventing sports injuries in children. We also thought it would be interesting to hear from a certified umpire, in this case Rich Nedimyer, about good sportsmanship and proper role modeling for young athletes. Finally, we wanted to offer the philosophies of Bob Bigelow, a former professional basketball player and an expert in adapting youth sports and coaching styles to maximize the natural way that youngsters learn through their own fun play.

On the next few pages, you'll find each of their thoughts and advice in their area of expertise. In some cases, you'll also notice that we've extended these experts' well respected points by merging their thoughts with the collective wisdom expressed by our hometown heroes.

Minimizing Sports Injuries in Players

There's nothing worse than losing a player to a senseless injury during the season. We've all seen the more common causes of injury in baseball – getting hit by the ball, sliding into bases improperly, colliding with another player, and so on. Fortunately, most of the time, these mishaps cause temporary discomfort to the player(s) involved. While some of these incidents are bound to occur, it is your responsibility as the coach (as well as the league's responsibility) to ensure that you are promoting safe game play as much as possible. There is simply no excuse for an injury caused by excessive repetition, regimentation, or overemphasis on winning.

Dr. Lyle J. Micheli *is the director of the Division of Sports Medicine at Boston Children's Hospital and Harvard Medical School and the past president of the American College of Sports Medicine. Besides his expertise as a world-renowned clinician and surgeon, Dr. Micheli's special interest in preventing, treating, and rehabilitating sports injuries in youth has been documented in his book* The Sports Medicine Bible for Young Athletes. *An interview with Dr. Micheli as well as a review of his book yielded several good tips on keeping kids safe and healthy when coaching youth baseball. We've included some excerpts here noting a few of his most relevant tips, but we refer you to his book for a full review of this subject.*

Injury prevention in baseball is a matter of coaches addressing key areas such as preparation, observing restrictions on overtraining, wearing proper protective equipment, and making appropriate adjustments to the playing environment.

❑ *Prepare players' bodies for exercise.*

Coaches should provide pre-season stretching and strengthening programs to assist in the prevention of overuse injuries associated with pitching.

Players should do stretching exercises and proper warm-ups before and after play. Stretching and strengthening routines are especially important in children because of their tendency to develop tight muscles, ligaments, and tendons during the growth process. Children's bones grow before their soft tissues do. That means that during growth spurts, muscles, ligaments, and tendons tend to get tighter and more vulnerable to injury.

❑ *Prevent overtraining for pitching or injury when sliding by using proper techniques.*

Coaches should set limits on the number of pitches thrown by a player per week, make rest periods between pitching mandatory, and teach proper pitching techniques.

• How many pitches are too many for a young player?

Dr. Micheli suggests that young baseball players should not perform more than 300 skilled throws a week, including those pitches thrown at practices and games, or they will dramatically increase their likelihood of developing osteochondritis ("Little League elbow"). He suggests that most leagues need to change their maximum six innings per week rule to a maximum pitches rule that includes pitches thrown in practice for more accurate tracking of pitch counts. His recommendation for tracking throws is to use a hand counter that can either be operated by coaches and/or by parent volunteers. Most leagues have pitching limit rules. But, you can always set your own team's pitching limits lower if you feel that the league's criteria are too relaxed.

- Why is throwing a curve ball so dangerous for children?

  A curve ball creates more torque on the player's arm due to the more horizontal, twisting motion required to make the pitch. This increases the possibility of damage to tendons and tissues surrounding the elbow.

- Where can you get information on proper pitching techniques?

  There are a wealth of good resources for teaching proper pitching technique in youth baseball. Check with your league to learn their recommendations. Also check for books and videos on the Internet at: http://www.amazon.com.

Players should be instructed to slide into bases in the proper manner. There is a detailed explanation of the proper body position for sliding in the "Water Sliding" Drill in Coaches' Favorite Drills.

❏ Use protective equipment.

Try to coach in leagues that provide this protective equipment for their teams.

- Players should always wear good quality, double-eared helmets with face protectors that protect the face from the tip of the nose to below the chin, including the teeth and facial bones.

- Catchers should always wear shin protection, athletic cups, chest plates, and helmets with masks.

❏ Create a safe playing environment.

Again, much of this safety advice is up to your league to implement. Exercise any option you may have for coaching in leagues that follow these guidelines.

- League officials should use breakaway/quick release bases instead of standard stationary bases to reduce the impact of a player sliding into base. Standard bases are not designed to absorb the force of a sliding player and can cause serious injuries to the hands and feet upon impact. According to Dr. Micheli, breakaway bases are associated with an 80% reduction in the risk of injury involved with sliding.

- Fences, walls, and posts should be padded to help prevent injury if players run into them when attempting to catch the ball.

- Protective screening should be used to protect players in dugouts and on benches.

- Playing fields and facilities should be well maintained.

- Safety screens should be used during practice, particularly for batting practice.

For more tips on youth sports health and safety consult Dr. Micheli's book:

Micheli, Lyle J., M.D. The Sports Medicine Bible for Young Athletes. 2001. Naperville, Illinois: Sourcebooks, Inc. 251pp. (www.sourcebooks.com)

An Umpire's Perspective

As a youth baseball coach, you will work with many umpires. You will watch them make many very good calls … and a handful of not so good ones. You will also experience many instances where the children and the parents on your team will look to you for modeling appropriate behavior towards umpires during games.

Youth league umpires, like other league volunteers, primarily spend their time at games to provide a positive sports experience for our children. But, conflicts often seem to arise regarding the proper way to interact with umpires when coaching a game. Our hometown hero coaches gave us very consistent advice on how to work effectively with umpires. We also thought it appropriate to offer some advice from an umpire's perspective.

Rich Nedimyer *is a certified umpire who has been calling games for over seven years. He has umpired at many levels and for many different leagues, including Little League®, Babe Ruth League®, the Clark C. Griffith Collegiate Baseball League® and Valley League Baseball, as well as for numerous high school games and NCAA Division I college games. Rich is a member of the Northern Virginia Baseball Umpires Association and the Mid Atlantic Collegiate (MAC) Umpires Association. He is also on the staff of the East Coast Athletic Conference. Rich provided us with his thoughts on umpiring, focusing on his experiences in youth leagues. We summarized several statements from our conversation with him.*

Rich feels that good sportsmanship includes understanding the rules of the contest, playing by those rules, and showing respect for both teammates and opponents. Above all, good sportsmanship means maintaining self-control at all times and always showing a positive attitude when cheering and coaching.

Rich reminds us that winning and losing lasts only a moment, but integrity and dignity are characteristics of a lifetime. He provides us with some of his own observations and suggestions to help coaches minimize conflicts and role model proper behavior for their players.

❏ *Keep control over your players.*

During games, coaches simply not having good control over their players can cause problems. Players using vulgar language on the field, complaining about ball and strike calls, and so on, should be addressed and corrected by coaches. Umpires appreciate it when a coach disciplines his or her players for doing these things. In addition, players are generally more receptive to being corrected by their own coach rather than by the umpire.

❏ *Learn the league rules.*

Many coaches at the youth level don't know the rules. An umpire doesn't mind being questioned on the interpretation of a rule, but many times coaches will argue a rule without having the correct facts.

❏ *Be cordial and personable to umpires.*

Umpires are taught to be cordial without appearing to be biased to one team or another. They are also taught to call coaches by their first names. It is a nice gesture for coaches to also call umpires by their first names on the field, rather than "Hey blue", or "Hey, ump".

❏ *Question calls in a civil manner. Be a positive role model.*

If a coach feels the need to question a call or rule interpretation, he or she should do it in a civil manner, rather than sprinting from the dugout to argue, or yelling from the dugout.

Kids in youth games generally follow the behavior of the coaches. If a coach is negative in his or her interactions with the umpire, then the kids will pick up on that and try to get away with the same negative behavior as well. A coach who is well-mannered will usually have well-mannered players.

In general, umpires will tend to tolerate less "bad behavior" in the youth leagues than in adult leagues. For instance, Rich would tend to be a little more lenient with behavior in a college game than a high school game. He, as most umpires, has very little tolerance for any kind of inappropriate behavior in youth games.

❑ *Never tolerate name-calling from your team's players or their parents.*

One thing that no umpire will tolerate is being a called a name. It is one thing for a coach to say, "That was a lousy call." It is quite another for a coach to say, "You are a lousy umpire". That will usually bring an immediate ejection from the game.

Parents and coaches should keep in mind that, no matter how good an umpire is, he or she is going to miss calls in every game. There is no rule in any baseball book that says that umpires are required to always get the calls right.

❑ *Keep the game event in perspective – for kids' sake.*

Everyone who is connected with youth baseball -- players, coaches, umpires, and parents -- should try to keep the whole experience in perspective. A youth baseball game is not a life and death situation. It should first and foremost be fun for the kids.

Parents and fans should remember to cheer for their team and not against the other team. Fan and parent reaction during a game should be positive at all times, and should not take the form of razzing the other team.

❑ *And now one for the umpires … hustle
and be enthusiastic!*

In Rich's opinion, the worst thing that an umpire can do in a game is not hustle. No matter what level of game he or she is working, it is important for the umpire to keep in mind that the game is still important to the players and coaches. Coaches and players deserve an umpire who hustles, looks his or her best, and is enthusiastic about what he or she is doing.

Adapting a Coaching Style for Children

Think back to your own sports experiences as a youngster. Chances are that your first thoughts are not about a particular coach you had … rather, they're about memorable events – a big hit or a great play you made, playing catch with your best friend, a silly joke that someone cracked while you were all sitting on the bench, and so on.

Now, think about the "good" coaches and the "bad" coaches who led your teams. Chances are that your impression of a "good" coach will closely correlate with how much involvement and fun you had during your season of play with that coach, and not how many games you won or lost.

Youngsters are motivated to participate in sports for reasons that may be very different from those of adult athletes. Young players tend to be motivated to play by getting to be on the same team with their friends, by being involved in games on a consistent basis, and especially by having fun.

As a youth baseball coach, you have a multi-faceted role to serve in coaching young players. Of course, you are expected to know and teach the rules of baseball. But, you must also be creative and look for ways to engage as many of the children on the team as possible in every practice and game. Most of all, you must challenge yourself to strive for making baseball fun at ANY level for ALL the players on your team.

Bob Bigelow *is a former NBA player, part-time NBA scout and youth coach who lectures across the country on how to restore a healthier perspective to youth sports. He has spent years researching the sociological, psychological, and physiological impacts of today's systems of youth sports. His book,* <u>Just Let the Kids Play: How to Stop Other Adults from Ruining Your Child's Fun and Success in Youth Sports</u> *outlines ways to set up teams that foster fair play, skill development, and social interaction. Mr. Bigelow offers a wealth of tips and advice for allowing children to enjoy sports the way they're supposed to, without sacrificing their chances at success. His full book is well worth the read, but following are some of his ideas you'll find particularly relevant to youth baseball.*

❏ *Strive for involvement for all players.*

Baseball is one of the most difficult youth games to coach because the nature of the game dictates that a number of players will wait while only one is at bat. For younger players this is a particularly difficult task, as their attention spans tend to be so short. That means that coaches must be creative and look for ways to engage as many of the children on the team as possible.

Here are some ideas that you might consider for different age groups. Implementing some of them will also require a commitment from your league, but they are still worth mentioning. As a coach, you can look to coach in leagues that subscribe to many of these ideas.

❑ *Create a highly active environment for 5- to 7-year-olds.*

Most children in baseball begin at young ages by playing the game of T-ball. The basic problem with T-ball is that too many coaches send nine or more players into the field to scoop up hits coming from one batter. Too many children are just watching, doing nothing, while a minority are active.

- Create a modified version of T-ball where three or four players are placed into the field while one bats at the tee. Have several of these games going on at once. Get more children moving and they won't be so bored. (If you can't implement this idea during a scheduled game, at least try it during a practice.)

- Hold no more than one event per week, not one game and one practice. At this level, there is no need to distinguish between games and practices. Just get together for a one-hour session and let the children play.

- Ask the children to keep score, not adults, or don't worry about keeping score at all. Don't compile team standings.

- Move young players around constantly. Never let them get so comfortable in one position that they won't try another.

- Start easing children off the tee in second grade and allow them to hit either adult pitches or balls shot from pitching machines.

❑ *Practice "minimum meaningful minutes" of playing time for 8- to 10-year-olds.*

After T-ball and machine or coach-pitch baseball, children enter the world of the kid-pitch, nine-on-the-field baseball team.

- As much as possible, provide every player with equal playing time and an equal chance to play all the positions. Commit to a policy of "minimum meaningful minutes" for every child on the team. *(The authors suggest that in order to learn to play in a game setting, a child should have a minimum of three full innings of play in each game, and more if possible.)*

- Some children will be uncomfortable pitching, catching and playing the infield. Do your best to recognize this and don't force children into doing so.

- Make practices last no more than one hour. *(Depending on the maturity of your team, you may be able to stretch your practices to 90 minutes for this age group. You should use your good judgment here.)* Begin with activities, but quickly get into an active scrimmage mode and move players around frequently. Playing the game is why the team showed up.

❑ *Continue to emphasize fair play and appropriate player involvement for 11- and 12-year-olds.*

Not a whole lot changes as children reach ages 11 or 12. A dozen players on a team still makes sense, as does a six-inning game, or ninety minutes, whichever comes first.

- Continue to move players around frequently to give them lots of experience at several positions.

- Keep practices to no longer than 90 minutes each. *(Again, depending on the maturity of your team, you may be able to stretch your practices to two hours for this age group. Use your best judgment.)*

- As children in this age group often move to playing on a larger diamond, take into account the time most players will need to adjust to the new dimensions.

❏ *Listen to your players and adjust your style accordingly.*

Not all teams you coach will require the same coaching style. Some groups of players will be more naturally advanced in their fundamental skills than others. Some teams will be more self-motivated than others. During the pre-season practices, listen to all members of your team and adjust your coaching style accordingly.

- Verbally poll the players to find out:

  - What is their favorite thing about playing baseball? Their least favorite?
  - How important is it for them to win games?
  - How important is it for them to play equal time?

Ask your players to suggest five ideas to make practices and games more fun.

- Verbally poll the players' parents to find out:

  - How many practices would they like to see this season?
  - Is there anything about their child that would be important for you, the coach, to understand?
  - How do parents define a successful season?

Ask the parents to suggest five ideas to make practices and games more fun.

Ask yourself as well about why you signed up to coach, your favorite and least favorite things about coaching, and how you will organize your team.

After gathering information from the polls, write a plan and a pledge to distribute to everyone, putting your commitments to coaching in writing. Your pledge can state how playing time will be divided, how positions will be assigned, and so on.

For more tips on promoting fair play and fun in youth sports, consult Bob Bigelow's book:

Bigelow, Bob, Moroney, T., and Hall, L. <u>Just Let the Kids Play: How to Stop Other Adults from Ruining Your Child's Fun and Success in Youth Sports.</u> 2001. Deerfield Beach, Florida: Health Communications, Inc. 336pp.

2

Coaches' Favorite Drills

In this section you will find a selection of our hometown heroes' favorite practice drills for youth baseball players. Our intention was not to provide you with the most comprehensive coverage of baseball drills for youth teams. There are several good sources for building your own comprehensive library of drills within other books, through your own league's practices, and on the Internet. Rather, we wanted to supplement your drills library by passing along the favorite drills mentioned by our hometown hero coaches as being the most successful for them. You should browse through this section and select those drills that may best pertain to your own particular coaching situation.

To assist you with rapid browsing, we have included in each drill our own arbitrary ratings for fun and fundamental skills (five "balls" or "bats" is highest) as well as a listing of appropriate age ranges. We have also used a baseball diamond diagram to provide a visual categorization of the type of skill being practiced by each drill. Finally, we have suggested some points in a "Coaching Analysis" for each drill to help you identify whether or not the drill is working well for your team's players.

Ready-Alligator-Crowhop

Contributed by John Mangieri
Davenport, Iowa

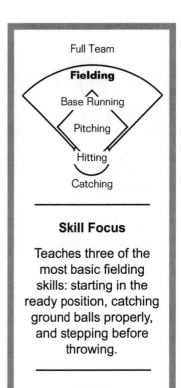

Full Team

Fielding

Base Running

Pitching

Hitting

Catching

Skill Focus

Teaches three of the most basic fielding skills: starting in the ready position, catching ground balls properly, and stepping before throwing.

Age Focus
5-10

Fun Rating

Fundamental Rating

It all starts with footwork. If the player's feet move quickly to get him into the proper position, as is the case in most sports, many positive things are possible. He's more likely to field the ball cleanly and make a strong, accurate throw if his feet are in the proper position.

☐ The Drill

Start by demonstrating the proper "ready position," which prepares the fielder for action. For infielders, the ready position has several key ingredients:

- FIELD POSITION – being in the right spot for the position (for example, the third baseman is normally about eight or ten feet from the base, just inside the imaginary baseline between second base and third base.)
- FEET – spread slightly wider than shoulder-width apart, leaning forward with bent knees.
- HANDS – open (palms up) and facing downward, as if ready to catch a beach ball.
- EYES – focused on the batter.
- MIND – thinking ahead, ready to make the appropriate play for the situation.

Next, comes the alligator. With the player in the ready position, he becomes an alligator, and his hands become the alligator's mouth. Roll a slow grounder to the player,

Coaching Analysis

After this drill, the coach should analyze the following:

- Did players consistently start each play in the ready position, as described herein?

- Did the "alligators" move their feet quickly to get into the proper position to "eat" the ball, with the throwing hand closing over the glove to form an "alligator's" mouth?

- After fielding or "eating" the baseball, did players grip the baseball properly, straighten from the crouched position, point the glove shoulder toward the target, and "crowhop" before throwing to the target?

and tell him to pretend he is an alligator, quickly moving his feet to get in front of the ball. As he moves aggressively to "eat the ball like an alligator," the glove goes down on the ground, and the throwing hand comes in to close like an alligator's jaws. There's a lower jaw (the glove) and an upper jaw (the throwing hand), closing on the ball like it's eating it.

Finally comes the crowhop. Treat it like a dance. Make a big deal out if it so the players remember it. It will put players in the proper throwing position, and it will force them not to rush the throw. After fielding the ball like alligator jaws, demonstrate the crowhop by hopping up and down, stepping toward the target, but not throwing the baseball. The key ingredients to the crowhop are:

- GRIP – grabbing the ball properly for a strong, accurate throw, moving the ball in the hand if necessary, so that the first two fingers are across the seams.
- STRAIGHTEN UP – from the crouched alligator fielding position, come up ready to make the throw.
- SHOULDER – point the glove shoulder toward the target (for example, first base, home plate, and so on).
- FEET – hop with both feet, landing first on the back foot, and then on the front foot as the throw is made to the target in the proper position, and with the proper leverage.

Once the players have mastered each of the three phases of this drill, put them all together. When each player is in the ready position, hit or roll a ground ball to them, have them move their feet quickly to get in front of the ball, field it like an alligator, and take a crowhop before making the throw.

Remember, it's more productive for young players to receive many slow grounders versus only a few hard grounders.

Hitting Off the Tee

Contributed by Rod Hudson
Gaithersburg, Maryland

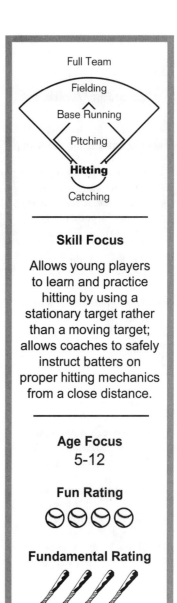

Full Team

Fielding

Base Running

Pitching

Hitting

Catching

Skill Focus

Allows young players to learn and practice hitting by using a stationary target rather than a moving target; allows coaches to safely instruct batters on proper hitting mechanics from a close distance.

Age Focus
5-12

Fun Rating

Fundamental Rating

The batting tee is an exceptional tool for players of all ages. The batting tee drill should continue even when the player becomes a major leaguer!

If your league does not provide a batting tee, we urge you to purchase one. In fact, we urge you to encourage all players to purchase a tee and use it whenever possible.

☐ The Drill

Set up a tee near the backstop, or use a portable "pop-up" hitting cage. Using tennis balls or plastic Whiffle® Balls, kneel next to the tee (in front of the batter, not behind him) and give instruction to each batter. By moving the batter and adjusting the rubber sleeve on the tee, you'll be able to simulate different pitch locations and hitting directions.

For inexperienced batters, start the drill by positioning the first batter appropriately at the tee, checking his grip, hand position, knee flex, feet position, and head position. One at a time, feed balls on the tee and have the batter take his stance, then stride and swing. After the swing, analyze the mechanics and make necessary adjustments. If the player misses the ball and hits the tee well below the ball, the bat may be too heavy for that particular player. Make sure the bat is comfortable for the player to swing quickly and smoothly.

Coaching Analysis

After this drill, the coach should analyze the following:

• Did the hitter have a good, balanced stance, with his hands, feet, head, knees, and bat in good ready position?

• Was the bat the proper weight for the hitter?

• Did the hitter have a good stride to start the swing?

• Did he keep his hands back until the swing began?

• Was his swing level?

• Did his hips open to allow the swing to come all the way through?

• Did his hands roll over to allow his hips and shoulders to rotate?

• Did he keep his head down and still, with eyes fixed on the ball?

The stride should only be six or eight inches for most players, and the swing should start a split second after the stride in order to maximize timing and strength. The hands should stay back and then come down and through. If the hands start forward too early and then have to come back to start the swing, it will be difficult to time the swing to match the speed of the pitch.

As the lead foot strides, the back foot pivots (called "squishing the bug"), the hips open (that is, rotate toward the pitcher), the head stays down and fixed on the ball, the hands bring the bat down and through the center of the ball, the hands roll after making contact, and the swing follows through with the bat ending up around the middle of the player's back. With each swing off the tee, adjust parts of the swing as necessary, particularly with the beginning batters.

Be careful not to over-coach an experienced batter. It won't be necessary to change the mechanics on every single swing. Particularly when players are experiencing some success off the tee, over-coaching may take away the confidence they've gained.

As players get comfortable hitting off the tee, position the tee for balls at the chest, at the knees, at the waist, and so on. Then, move the player's feet and have them try to hit the ball inside, outside, down the line, to the opposite field, and up the middle. Prior to batting in real "batting practice" or in games, have players hit off the tee. Have them practice at home every chance they get. It will be worth it.

Bean Bag Catch

Contributed by Lloyd Rue
Helena, Montana

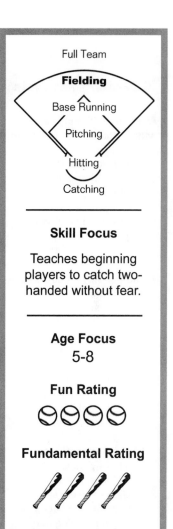

Full Team

Fielding
Base Running
Pitching
Hitting
Catching

Skill Focus

Teaches beginning players to catch two-handed without fear.

Age Focus
5-8

Fun Rating

Fundamental Rating

Almost all kids, even experienced players, are afraid of the baseball. To eliminate some of that fear, introduce T-ballers through 8-year-olds to baseballs by way of bean bags. Kids are generally unafraid of bean bags, so they won't shy away from them as they're learning to catch with two hands. This is a great drill for the first practice of the season.

☐ The Drill

Have a handful of players spread out in a line, side-by-side, with plenty of space between each of the players. Have parents or assistant coaches match up with one or two players each, moving back to a distance where the kids can still succeed (start at about ten feet and move back from there).

Without gloves, the players will be catching bean bags with two hands. They should start in the ready position, with open hands (as though they are catching an imaginary beach ball just below waist level), slightly bent knees, feet about shoulder width apart, and alert eyes. Since anything thrown overhand looks intimidating to a 5- or 6-year-old, have the coaches and parents throw the bean bags underhanded to each player, instructing them to move both hands to catch the bean bag. Try to make the first four throws directly to the players.

Coaching Analysis

After this drill, the coach should analyze the following:

- Did players begin each catch in the ready position?

- Did they field the bean bags in a balanced position?

- Did the players use both hands to make each catch, keeping their eyes trained on the bean bag?

- On bean bags thrown in front of their feet, did players keep their hands down on the ground to make the catch without pulling up?

- Most importantly, do you have a sense after completing the drill that players have developed the confidence necessary to begin catching real baseballs with two hands?

As individual players become comfortable catching the bean bags with both hands, start tossing them over their heads and to the sides, forcing the kids to move their feet. Encourage foot movement, even when the bean bag is thrown right to them. On throws above a player's head, try to get him used to catching with bent elbows and with one foot back slightly for better balance.

Next, have the players assume the gorilla ready position from about 20 feet away. Have the parents or assistant coaches throw the bean bags sidearm just in front of the players' feet. Since bean bags tend to slide instead of skip or bounce, the players will be forced to keep their gloves and hands down on the ground in order to catch the bean bags. Teaching players to stay down on ground balls will be one of the most difficult challenges you'll face as a coach, and the Bean Bag Catch will make the challenge easier without the fear of a real baseball.

A great variation of the Bean Bag Catch can be accomplished by performing the drill blindly. Partner the kids together in groups of two players. The partner who is going to catch the bean bag should be facing forward, with the other partner standing about five feet behind him. The player from behind tosses the bean bag straight up over the head of the front player, who in turn tries to catch it without tilting his head back. As soon as the bean bag enters the front player's line of sight, he moves from the ready position to catch it with both hands. This drill (both versions) will develop much needed confidence in younger kids, but it will still be a fun challenge.

For more experienced players, try using actual baseballs in the blind version of this drill.

Gorilla Grounders & Gorilla Races

Contributed by Steve Wagner
DeMotte, Indiana

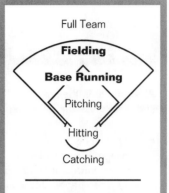

Full Team

Fielding

Base Running

Pitching

Hitting

Catching

Skill Focus

Emphasizes the importance of starting in the ready position and staying down when fielding grounders.

Age Focus
5-10

Fun Rating

Fundamental Rating

Have you ever seen an infielder who's in the ready position or fielding a ground ball? He looks kind of like a gorilla, leaning over with his arms hanging down and open in the middle. To emphasize the importance of the ready position and fielding position, this drill exaggerates the posture and makes it fun. For youngsters, tedious fundamentals can be easier to remember when you do something fun with them.

☐ The Drill

Before beginning Gorilla Grounders, demonstrate the proper ready position, exaggerating the posture and even throwing in some gorilla grunts and movements. Make it

fun! Now, one at a time, have each player do his best gorilla impression (with his glove on). This is a great opportunity to single out one of the shy, inexperienced players by telling him how awesome his "gorilla" is, which may give him a little extra encouragement.

Next, have a few parents or assistant coaches roll

Coaching Analysis

After this drill, the coach should analyze the following:

• Did players get into an exaggerated ready position, with crouched body, open hands, spread feet, hanging arms, and bent knees?

• Did players have enough fun with the gorilla grounders and gorilla races to remember the gorilla ready position?

grounders to each player, two or three players at a time, encouraging them to start in the "gorilla" ready position. Make sure players have low, open hands, feet spread at least shoulder width apart, knees bent and waist bent so that they can scoop the dirt with their gloves. Continue to roll grounders to each player in the gorilla position. Encourage the kids to be animated and have fun with it. The more fun they have, the more likely they are to remember to stay in the ready position and field grounders like a gorilla.

When the players have the hang of it, line them all up at home plate, and have them race "gorilla style" around the bases. Again, encourage the kids to have as much fun as they can with the races.

During the subsequent games, yell to the players, "You don't look much like gorillas to me," and the players will likely smile and get into the ready position.

Fielding From the Knees

Contributed by Monie Duran
San Dimas, California

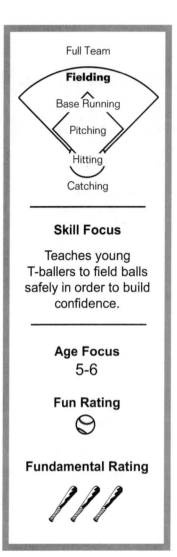

Full Team

Fielding

Base Running

Pitching

Hitting

Catching

Skill Focus

Teaches young
T-ballers to field balls
safely in order to build
confidence.

Age Focus
5-6

Fun Rating

Fundamental Rating

For beginning players of T-ball age, it is important to safely build confidence before doing anything else. Remember that most players at this age will have no experience and very little confidence when it comes to fielding. Some won't even know which hand the glove goes on. In fact, to start this drill, gloves aren't even necessary.

This drill is ideal for the first practice of the season. Try to encourage all parents to stay for the first practice. Their help will be useful with the drill and the kids will feel more comfortable in their presence. Practicing with a parent (or another adult) at this level works well because children this young need one-on-one attention since this is usually new to them.

☐ The Drill

Start with about six players, while the remaining players work on other simple skill development (running, throwing, and so on). Have parents work with their own kids, lining up directly across from them, about five or six feet away.

Start the drill using tennis balls and without gloves. Have the players kneel down in the ready position, with their bare hands down and open. Instruct the parents to toss the tennis balls softly to their player so that catches are made out in front of the body between the thighs and chest, with both hands coming together to grasp the ball. Be sure to

Coaching Analysis

After this drill, the coach should analyze the following:

- Did the kids keep their eyes on the tosses, watching the ball all the way into the hands or glove?

- Did the kids hold their gloves appropriately for the different types of tosses, particularly holding them upright on tosses above the chest?

- Did each player show confidence when progressing through each level of the drill to the point where you feel comfortable introducing them to other defensive drills with real baseballs?

notice whether or not the players are watching the ball all the way into their hands. By catching several tennis balls with "open" bare hands, the players will develop confidence without the safety risk of using real baseballs.

Once the kids are comfortable catching the ball "out front," let the players know that the next throws will be near their heads. Instruct them to turn their hands up in order to catch the ball and protect their faces. When they are comfortable catching balls at their heads, have them put on their gloves, but continue throwing tennis balls instead of baseballs. On the throws at the head, make sure players still watch the ball all the way into the glove. This may take some time.

Of equal importance is the position of the glove. By having the kids stay on their knees, it will force them to turn the glove upright on throws higher then the chest. Continue to remind young players to keep their gloves upright (with the heel down and the web and fingers up) on higher throws. This simple skill will be important as you introduce baseballs to the drill.

Use soft-cover baseballs (reduced injury factor baseballs) while players are still kneeling. Once players get more confident, begin to toss the ball away from their bodies and heads, showing them to how to hold the glove for tosses to either side. Eventually (perhaps at the next practice), have the players stand to catch short tosses. Remember, safety and confidence are important at this level. Don't be afraid to go slowly when progressing from kneeling and catching tennis balls with bare hands to standing and catching baseballs with gloves.

Hit the Tarp Progressive Pitching

Contributed by Bill Sandry
Bettendorf, Iowa

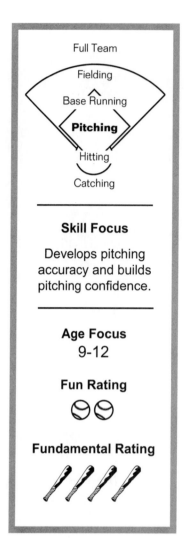

Skill Focus

Develops pitching accuracy and builds pitching confidence.

Age Focus
9-12

Fun Rating

Fundamental Rating

Teaching a young player to be a pitcher is one of the most difficult challenges a coach faces. Other players on the field occasionally feel pressure when they react to a hit ball or a base stealer, but the pitcher faces significant pressure to hit a small target (a catcher's mitt) on every single pitch. That's a hard thing to do at any level, but it's especially difficult for youngsters. Having to focus on too many things (the target, the distance, the throwing mechanics, the batter, the count, the base runners) makes it even more challenging. Start off by building a pitcher's confidence before developing his mechanics.

Start slowly. Make the distance shorter and the target bigger until you have a chance to develop the player's mechanics and confidence. Then, gradually increase the target challenge.

☐ The Drill

Buy a canvas or heavy gauge vinyl tarp (approximately four feet by six feet or five feet by eight feet), and paint a rectangular strike zone on it approximately 20-24 inches wide (to expand the zone a bit), and 3 to 4 feet high. Attach it to the backstop so that the bottom of the strike zone is about a foot or so off the ground.

At first, the entire tarp is the target. Read your league's rulebook to get the appropriate age group distance from the pitching rubber to home plate. If that distance is 46 feet, start this drill at a manageable distance of about 30 or 40 feet. All the players have to worry about is hitting the tarp. Try not to focus too much on mechanics until the pitcher has developed the confidence and accuracy to hit the tarp.

Once he has mastered that (for say, eight out of ten pitches), change pitchers. Again, have the pitchers simply focus on hitting the tarp. As the pitchers gain confidence, change your coaching focus to their basic mechanics (balance, arm

position, stride, finish, and so on). As you work with them on mechanical techniques, they should still focus on hitting the tarp, not yet "aiming" for the strike zone.

After each pitcher has successfully hit the tarp with some consistency, instruct them to change their focus to the marked strike zone. Again try not to worry too much about specific mechanics. The primary focus of this drill is to give potential pitchers the confidence to go to the next step toward becoming a pitcher.

Offer lots of praise during this phase of the drill, even if many pitches are a little outside the marked strike zone. Remember, many "close" pitches will become called strikes or missed swings during game situations.

In later practices, you will have opportunities to address specific mechanical deficiencies. For this drill, the point is to develop confidence in young players who may have the desire or aptitude to pitch.

Keep in mind that young pitchers should only throw a maximum of 300 pitches a week, including those throws made in games and at practices. (Refer to Dr. Lyle Micheli's sports safety information in "Advice From the Experts" in Coaches' Tips & Advice.

Coaching Analysis

After this drill, the coach should analyze the following:

- Were pitchers able to successfully hit the tarp, regardless of mechanical form?

- After successfully hitting the tarp, were pitchers able to hit the marked strike zone on the tarp with some success?

- After completing the drill, were pitchers left with the confidence to want to continue pitching?

Bunting for Dollars

Contributed by Mike Miselis
Bayonne, New Jersey

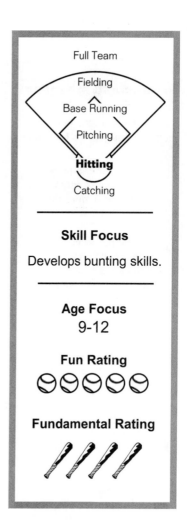

Full Team

Fielding

Base Running

Pitching

Hitting

Catching

Skill Focus

Develops bunting skills.

Age Focus
9-12

Fun Rating

Fundamental Rating

How many kids voluntarily square around to bunt without being told to do so? The term "never" comes to mind. By offering a little incentive, 9-year-olds and up should be encouraged to develop their bunting skills, a dying art in baseball. There's nothing more exciting to watch than a kid laying down a great bunt. A player may go up against the greatest pitcher in the world, and be totally outmatched, but he may find a way to beat that pitcher by laying down a great bunt.

☐ The Drill

To add incentive and make bunting fun for the players, pull out a dollar bill and place it on the spot where a great bunt would land. For right-handed batters, the spot would be toward the third baseman, about 15 or 20 feet from home plate. For lefties, the ideal spot would be toward the first baseman, about 20 feet from home plate. Before beginning, have the pitcher (in this case, a coach) move closer to the plate, about 30 to 40 feet away from the batters, so that the players will be less intimidated. Pitch enough slow balls for each batter to lay down five or six bunts, and mark the best one. It's important to have one of your assistant coaches pitch this drill, so that you can focus on the batter's bunting technique.

At this age, when players are just learning the bunt, they should be focusing on "sacrificing" themselves to advance

Coaching Analysis

After this drill, the coach should analyze the following:

- Did the batter square around completely to face the pitcher before the windup?

- Did the batter use the proper bunting technique with hands forward and parallel, knees bent, eyes on the ball, and hands pulled back to "deaden" the ball?

- Did the drill encourage weaker hitters/bunters?

other base runners, and consequently, should be squaring around before the pitching motion starts. Learning to bunt for a base hit will come later in a player's development.

Have each batter bunt five or six balls, letting each ball come to a complete stop. Then mark the spot or record a measurement for the ball that landed closest to the dollar bill. After all the players have had a chance to lay down some bunts, award the dollar to the player whose bunt came closest to the money. You may end up with a "rightie" winner and a "leftie" winner. If the ball comes to a stop on the bill, you may want to offer a $5 bonus, or a $10 gift certificate at a sporting goods store.

Encourage batters to exhibit proper bunting techniques, including:

- sliding the top hand to the fat part of the bat barrel, holding the bat on the back side with the thumb and first two fingers <u>behind</u> the bat.
- holding the hands forward so that the bat is extended and the elbows are almost straight.
- keeping the knees slightly bent.
- watching the ball all the way to contact.
- keeping the bat parallel when moving it up or down with the pitch.
- pulling the hands back slightly just before contact to "deaden" the ball.
- making sure both feet are spread apart, facing the pitcher, inside the batter's box until contact is made. (Many coaches will prefer a staggered stance, but we recommend a square stance for the first few years of a player's bunting development.)

Two-Ball Grounder

Contributed by Colonel John Parker
Hilton Head, South Carolina

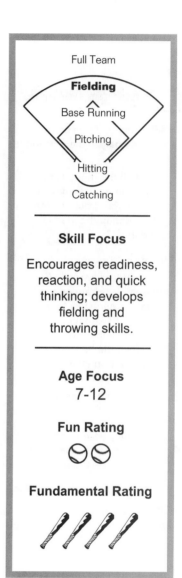

Full Team

Fielding
Base Running
Pitching
Hitting
Catching

Skill Focus

Encourages readiness, reaction, and quick thinking; develops fielding and throwing skills.

Age Focus
7-12

Fun Rating

Fundamental Rating

Hitting tons of ground balls has always been a staple of baseball practice at any level. Muscle memory and repetition are important developmental elements of learning in any sport. To an 8-year-old, though, catching grounders over and over can be a little tedious. The two-ball drill includes the repetition of fielding grounders, but it goes a little bit beyond that by incorporating quick thinking with the addition of the second ball. It's simple, but effective.

☐ The Drill

Have players line up at the infield positions, including pitcher and catcher. When the third baseman is in the ready position, hit a ground ball in his direction. That player should field the ball properly and then throw to the second baseman, who has moved to cover the base (make sure that the throw goes over the base, not to the player covering the base.) The second baseman then throws the ball hard to the catcher. As that ball is being thrown home, hit a second ground ball to the same third baseman, who should field the ball properly and throw to the first baseman, again throwing hard to the base, not to the player.

As that second ball is being thrown home, immediately hit a ground ball in the neighborhood of the shortstop, who fields it and throws to the second baseman covering the base. As he throws home, immediately hit a second ball to

Coaching Analysis

After this drill, the coach should analyze the following:

• Did all the players, not just the ones fielding a particular grounder, stay focused in the ready position?

• Did players field grounders properly (for example, charging the ball, staying low to the ground, keeping the glove down, using "soft" hands to field the ball, coming up to a hop step position, throwing a line drive to the head of the target position player)?

• Did players cover the appropriate bases at the appropriate times?

the same shortstop, who throws to the first baseman, who again throws home.

Now, hit a grounder to the second baseman, who throws the ball home to the catcher. Again, as that ball is coming home, hit a second ball to the second baseman, who throws to the shortstop covering second base.

Next, hit grounders to the first baseman who throws to the player at third base and second base, respectively. Then hit two balls to the pitcher, and then the catcher, who each throw to second base and first base. After the catcher's second throw, have players switch with the next round of infielders for the same drill.

This drill forces players to stay in the ready position for both grounders, demands foot movement to cover bases, and forces players to think and react to each grounder, whether it's hit to them or not.

Whiffle® Ball Soft Toss

Contributed by Tom Allen
North East, Maryland

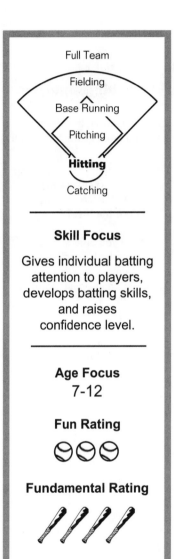

Skill Focus

Gives individual batting attention to players, develops batting skills, and raises confidence level.

Age Focus
7-12

Fun Rating

Fundamental Rating

What typically drives young kids away from the game isn't so much their ability to field as it is their ability to hit. If youngsters fail at hitting or become afraid of the ball, they are often inclined to give up on the game altogether. Soft toss, particularly with plastic Whiffle® Balls, is really a tremendous drill that can and should be used repeatedly at any age level above T-ball. You can't just toss a beginner in the batting cage or batter's box and expect them to hit real baseballs. By working with them one-on-one, with unintimidating plastic balls, you can focus on their batting skills and help them develop much needed confidence.

☐ The Drill

While other players are working at other drills or skill stations, have one or two kids hit soft-toss plastic balls into a fence or backstop. Position the player about ten feet away from the backstop or fence in a normal batter's stance, with a home plate or something to represent the home plate. Kneel down across from the plate, facing the plate, not the batter. Advise the batter to be prepared to swing quickly in a downward, compact motion. For the batter, the objective of this drill is to make contact with an efficient, compact swing. For the coach, the objective of this drill is to communicate face-to-face with each player, offering mechanical instruction and psychological encouragement.

Coaching Analysis

After this drill, the coach should analyze the following:

- Were hitters able to swing quickly, keeping their hands back and locked before the toss?

- Were you able to help hitters with specific skills or faults (e.g., hip pivot, head position, stepping in the bucket, and so on?)

- Did weaker hitters develop more confidence as a result of the drill and your verbal encouragement?

Begin by tossing balls directly over the plate, about waist high, so that the batter can quickly swing and hit the ball into the fence. Try to focus on several things during this drill:

- the batter should keep his hands back, locked and ready to swing, not forward and then back.
- The swing should be fixed so that it contacts the ball as the toss reaches its apex if possible. This skill may take time to develop in younger players.
- If it helps the batter to swing through the zone quickly, have him squish the bug with his back foot before he gets locked and ready to swing.
- This is a great opportunity to ensure that batters are swinging slightly downward and not upper-cutting.
- The batter should stride only a few inches with the lead foot, directly toward the fence.
- If he is struggling to get the bat through the zone quickly, but he has his hands back and has already squished the bug and is locked and loaded, encourage him to try a lighter bat.
- If necessary, adjust your tosses so that weaker batters can make contact more easily.
- Continue to offer positive encouragement as often as possible, especially to weaker batters.

For better batters, try using plastic golf balls or cheap ping-pong balls, forcing them to concentrate more effectively in order to make contact with a smaller ball. Tossing plastic balls underhanded (large or small) should give you a great opportunity to focus on batting skill development and build confidence.

Be careful not to over-coach young batters. It won't be necessary to change the mechanics on every single swing. Particularly when players are experiencing some success off the tee, over-coaching may take away the confidence they've gained. Remember that encouraging young batters to swing, even if it's an ugly swing, is your primary goal.

Running Through First Base

Contributed by Monie Duran
San Dimas, California

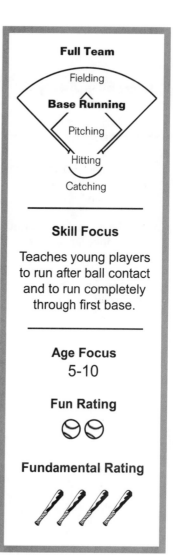

Full Team

Fielding

Base Running

Pitching

Hitting

Catching

Skill Focus

Teaches young players to run after ball contact and to run completely through first base.

Age Focus
5-10

Fun Rating

Fundamental Rating

How many times have you seen a youth baseball player start running to first base and slow down before he gets there, only to stop on the base or to be thrown out because he slowed down too soon? Even experienced players sometimes make this mistake. Running through first base is one of those simple, but essential skills that needs to be engrained in players at a very young age.

☐ The Drill

Some youth leagues use a safety base at first base (see photo on next page), which serves to prevent dangerous collisions on close plays. If the fields in your community don't provide such bases, set up your own safety base beside the regular first base, but outside the foul line. This safety base will serve as the target for the runner, and the regular base will be the foot base for the first baseman.

Make sure both bases are staked securely in the ground so that they won't slip when players step on them during the drill. Check with your league representative regarding the proper distance from the back point of home plate to the edge of each base (usually 60 or 70 feet for most youth leagues). Once the bases are staked into the ground, line up every player behind home plate.

As the first player gets into the ready position inside the batter's box area, have another coach yell "go," which will

Coaching Analysis

After this drill, the coach should analyze the following:

- Did the players keep their eyes on the base and the base coach?

- Did the players slow down before they got to their goal?

- Did they turn toward foul territory (to the right) after running through the base?

signify that the batter has made contact with the pitch and that the ball is being fielded on the ground and thrown to first base. The runner should immediately sprint full-speed

to the outer (safety) base at first base, not slowing down or looking around in the process. You should be stationed in the first base coach's box, yelling for the player to run "through" the base, and the player should be looking only at the base and you. The player should not slow down at all until three or four steps <u>after</u> he reaches the base, at which point he should be taught to turn toward foul territory, not toward fair territory. This is critical!

After the first runner runs "through" first base, be sure to let him know if he slowed down too early or looked around in any direction other than first base as he was running. Have the other coach again yell "go," signaling the next player to sprint from the batter's box to the outer first base, slowing down only after stepping on first.

Run the entire team through this drill three or four times. When it appears that most players understand the concept of running through the base, introduce a batting tee, a few infielders (adults), and a first baseman (this could be a player). Now have the players put on a helmet and hit an intentional grounder off the tee. After they make contact, they should drop (not throw) the bat, and sprint to the outer first base. Make sure they don't look at the ball or the fielders as they are running, and make sure they again don't slow down until they get through the base.

When a ball and a few fielders are introduced to the drill, there will be a tremendous temptation for players to turn their heads to look at the action. It's imperative that they focus only on the base and the coach.

Middle of the Circle

Contributed by Bob Karol
Wayland, Massachusetts

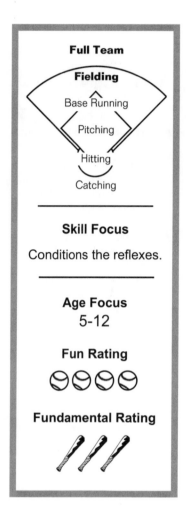

Full Team

Fielding

Base Running

Pitching

Hitting

Catching

Skill Focus

Conditions the reflexes.

Age Focus
5-12

Fun Rating

Fundamental Rating

This drill is for reflexes. It's fun because it becomes a game instead of a drill, and it involves the entire team. Any drill that moves quickly and keeps every player involved and focused is a necessity for a coach.

☐ The Drill

Have all the players form a circle around you, in the ready position with gloves in hand, with about three or four feet between each player. Start the drill by looking directly at a player and rolling a slow grounder in his direction. (For T-ballers, call the player's name before you roll the ball.) The player should field the ball properly, with crouched stance,

Coaching Analysis

After this drill, the coach should analyze the following:

• Did the players stay alert in the ready position, even when the ball was rolled to someone else?

• Did they field each grounder in a crouched position, with open hands, gloves held low to the ground, watching the ball all the way into their gloves?

open hands, appropriate foot movement, glove held low to the ground, and so on. Then the player should take a crow-hop and throw the ball back to you in the center of the circle. Next, look at a different player and roll a ground ball toward him. Again, the player should field the ball properly, take a crow-hop, and throw back to you.

After the first few rounds, as the players get comfortable with the drill, mix things up by rolling to a player you're NOT looking at or even a player behind you. If a player misses the ball, he's out. As players are eliminated, have them go to another station for a different activity.

It becomes a game instead of a drill. For 11- and 12-year-olds, you may even throw a few soft line drive tosses instead of grounders, just to keep players alert. On the line drive throws, players should catch balls above the waist with gloves pointed up (web facing up and heel facing down). The last player in the circle wins!

You may even try two baseballs at once, or two coaches in the middle of the circle, each possibly with two baseballs.

Catching the Foxtail®

Contributed by the Authors

This drill develops eye-hand coordination and encourages foot movement, which is often the most important and overlooked physical skill in any team sport. The Foxtail® is a soft leather ball (slightly smaller than a baseball) that is sewn onto three colored segments of nylon fabric that make up the "tail." It's not nearly as hard as a baseball, so it won't hurt if the player misses it.

☐ The Drill

Each player takes a turn, beginning in the ready position and facing the coach from about 20 feet away. Holding near the end of the tail, the coach throws the Foxtail® to the player in an underhand softball pitch motion, first swinging your arm backward, and then releasing it forward so that it sails into the air like a soft pop-up. From the ready position, the player takes a quick step backward, then moves his feet to run toward the direction of the Foxtail®. As he gets into position under it, square to the ball (not sideways) he extends his glove hand (but without the glove). Instead of catching the ball, he concentrates on catching just behind the ball in the first colored segment of the tail (on my Foxtail®, this section is pink).

Many young players don't train their eyes on the balls and watch them all the way into their gloves. This drill forces young players to focus their eyes intently on the area (and color) just behind the actual ball, training their eyes to follow

Full Team

Fielding

Base Running

Pitching

Hitting

Catching

Skill Focus

Develops eye-hand coordination; encourages foot movement.

Age Focus
7-12

Fun Rating

Fundamental Rating

Coaching Analysis

After this drill, the coach should analyze the following:

• Did the player start in the ready position?

• Was his first step back (as it should always be on a fly ball)?

• Did he move his feet quickly to get to the Foxtail®, or were his feet "lazy," causing him to be late getting to the Foxtail®?

• When he got to the Foxtail®, was he in good position to make the catch (as opposed to standing sideways, perhaps afraid to get hit by the Foxtail®)?

• Did he catch the Foxtail® in the first colored segment nearest the ball (the ideal outcome), or in a segment further from the ball (less desirable), or did he miss the catch altogether?

• Did his eyes appear to follow the Foxtail® all the way through the catch?

the ball all the way until the catch is made, developing their eye-hand coordination as it relates to catching fly balls.

Once kids have mastered the Foxtail® catch, move back another 30 or 40 feet, and begin throwing higher pop-ups. Again, encourage immediate foot movement so that players can get themselves into position to make the catch. Remember, on pop-ups, the first step must always be backwards. Then, the player will adjust and run in the direction of the Foxtail® (and eventually the baseball) to make the play.

Variation: Once your players have mastered the Foxtail® catch, play a game of team Foxtail® (kind of like Ultimate Frisbee®). Split up into even teams (perhaps include some of the parents) and make end zones. Players move down the field, passing the Foxtail® to each other, attempting to get into the end zone. A legal catch is made when the player catches only the tail section without contacting the ball.

NOTE:

If you are unable to locate a Foxtail® (made by Klutz Company), you may improvise. Take a few old tube socks and a baseball. Wrap the baseball in a sock or two, then put it into another tube sock. Tie another sock in a knot onto that one, then another one, and so on. You can make it as long as you'd like, but anything longer than four feet may be too long for younger kids.

Base Running Relay Race

Contributed by Dennis Dunn
Olney, Maryland

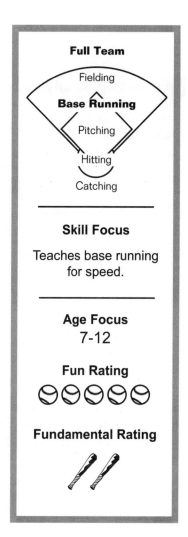

Full Team

Fielding

Base Running

Pitching

Hitting

Catching

Skill Focus

Teaches base running for speed.

Age Focus
7-12

Fun Rating

Fundamental Rating

Need an excuse to have kids carry all the equipment to your car? Need a reason to run the players into the ground to get rid of all their energy? Then, this is your drill!

☐ The Drill

Line up half your players at home plate and half at second base. The first player at home plate is facing first base, starting behind or on the plate. The first player at the second base line is facing third base, starting behind or on the base. As you yell "go," the first player from each line sprints toward the next base (third base for the line at second, and first base for the line at home plate), touches the base, and continues to the next bases. When the first players reach their starting points, they step on the base or plate and continue running through to allow the next player in line to take off behind them. The second players run around the base paths, hitting each base and continuing back to the original base or plate. The race continues until each player has made it all the way around and back to the starting point. The "team" that completes the race first wins.

To add some extra excitement to the race, include a few coaches or parents. Try your best to make teams even, based not only on raw speed, but also on base running (particularly "rounding") skill. To add incentive to the drill, have the losing team round up all the equipment and carry it to the coach's car.

Coaching Analysis

After this drill, the coach should analyze the following:

- Did you create evenly matched teams? If not, adjust the teams accordingly for a second race.

- Did all players touch each and every base? If not, they should be instructed to go back during the race and touch any bases they missed.

- Did players wait until the previous runner crossed the base or plate in front of them?

- Did both teams have fun? This should be a fun drill.

Grip, Balance & Foot Location

Contributed by Richard Nagata
Aiea, Hawaii

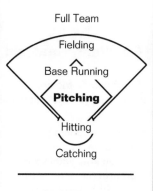

Skill Focus

Teaches pitchers progressive balance techniques, the importance of grip and release, and proper stride foot landing location.

Age Focus
11-12

Fun Rating

Fundamental Rating

Balance is the key! Many beginning coaches often make the mistake of giving the chance to pitch only to their hardest throwers. Even a 12-year-old who hasn't pitched at all can be an effective pitcher if he possesses basic mechanical skills and good balance.

☐ The Drill

Start by demonstrating the proper grip for pitchers. With pitchers under 12, teach a 4-seam grip, with the fingers holding the baseball <u>across</u> the seams for better accuracy. At about 13 and up, pitchers may choose to experiment with 2-seam grips <u>on</u> the seams, with different thumb placements and pressures placed on the ball for movement on the pitches. For this drill, stick with the 4-seam grip, reminding pitchers to relax their wrists and release the ball off their fingertips. If the grip is too tight on the baseball, the release will get locked up, creating speed and accuracy deficiencies. The wrist should be loose, the fingertips should be across the seams, and the release should roll off the fingertips.

Start off this throwing activity with three or four pitching prospects paired with three or four parents or coaches to catch for them while remaining players are occupied at other skill stations. With both knees on the ground and square to the parent or coach catcher (about 20 or 30 feet away), have each player make 10-12 very controlled throws, using very basic mechanics.

Coaching Analysis

After this drill, the coach should analyze the following:

- Did the pitchers limit themselves to the movements within each progressive step of the drill, from starting with both knees on the ground and using little body movement to ending with the full windup motion?

- Did they use the proper 4-seam grip, loosely held, with a fingertip release? If not, work exclusively on hand and wrist mechanics before allowing that pitcher to move to the next pitching activity.

- Did they end the full windup with the lead foot pointed toward the target?

- Throughout the drill, did the pitchers maintain good balance? If not, concentrate exclusively on making minor adjustments to help with balance (for example, shorter stride, less exaggerated movements, and so on.)

Next, have each pitcher put his left foot forward (if he is right-handed), with the knee at 90 degrees and the toes pointed to the catcher, again, for 10-12 throws. Then, have each pitcher stand and increase the distance between himself and his catcher, but with both feet together, not striding during the throws. This will force him to torque the trunk of his body as he winds up and untorque for the release.

After 10 or 12 throws with the feet together, instruct each pitcher to stride with the lead foot (left foot for right-handers), landing with the toes pointed toward the target. Finally, each pitcher should be instructed to increase his throwing distance and use a full windup for the last set of throws. (For detailed pitching mechanics, refer to "Word Association Pitching" in Coaches' Favorite Drills.) Remember to observe the grip, release, balance, and foot location with the full windup.

Tennis Ball Progressive Hitting

Contributed by Tom Sutton
Germantown, Maryland

Ideal for early season practices, the tennis ball progressive hitting drill can be used in bad weather conditions, on a tennis court, or on a basketball court, if necessary. Do you have a practice scheduled in early March on what ends up being a rainy day? Have the kids show up at a public hard court of some sort. Bring lots of tennis balls and a batting tee. By using tennis balls instead of real baseballs, weather won't be an issue, and young players will be in a position to gain hitting confidence without experiencing the fear some kids face.

☐ The Drill

This drill is run in three segments or stations. Explain each of the stations before the drill begins. Station 1 will have three or four players hitting tennis balls off the batting tee while other players are stretching or performing another poor-weather exercise. Before each of the Station 1 players hits off the tee, have them stretch with the bat and take some practice swings. You should correct only glaring imperfections at this time.

Once the players begin hitting off the tee, use your judgment in correcting any mechanical deficiencies. Since this drill is often utilized early in the season, it's probably a good opportunity to reconstruct the swings of beginners and tweak the swings of more experienced batters. If some

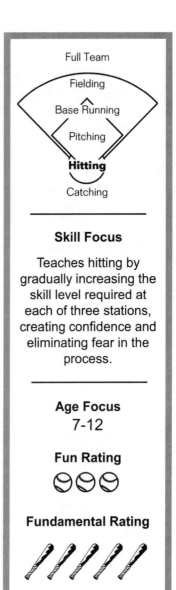

Full Team
Fielding
Base Running
Pitching
Hitting
Catching

Skill Focus

Teaches hitting by gradually increasing the skill level required at each of three stations, creating confidence and eliminating fear in the process.

Age Focus
7-12

Fun Rating

Fundamental Rating

Coaching Analysis

After this drill, the coach should analyze the following:

- Did all hitters effectively stretch and prepare themselves prior to Station 1?

- Did hitters at Station 1 use proper swing mechanics (that is, hand position, feet position, stride, level swing, hip rotation, and so on), and did they adjust properly to critical instruction from the Station 1 coach? If not, consider individual swing instruction for any such hitters.

- Were hitters able to hit with confidence by the time they reached Station 3? For any players who still appear to show signs of fear by the time they reach the coach-pitch station, try having them go back to Station 2, where they hit a moving target without the fear of being hit by a pitch. Even with tennis balls, there may be a player or two who will still show some signs of fear, particularly through ages nine or ten.

batters are not able to adjust their swings properly, perhaps individualized instruction is in order.

Upon completing Station 1, players move to Station 2, where a coach throws soft toss, again using tennis balls. While the players at Station 2 are hitting soft-tossed balls into a fence, three or four other players will begin at Station 1, the tee station. Station 2, like Station 1, should be used as an instructional tool. The coach who is throwing soft-toss will be close enough to the hitters to observe positive and negative swing characteristics, and offer appropriate praise and/or constructive instruction. Remember to offer more praise than criticism, especially for weak batters.

After three sets of about 15 or 20 swings per batter at each station, batters from Station 1 move to Station 2, and players from Station 2 go to Station 3 to complete the coach-pitch segment of the drill. The coach with the most accurate pitching arm (at slow speeds) should pitch tennis balls to batters at Station 3. By the time players reach this station, they ideally will have worked out the major problems with swing mechanics, and more importantly, they will have gained significant confidence. With the confidence they've gained, and with fear not being a factor, batters will likely do better at the coach-pitch station than they would if they were just thrown into a batting cage early in the season.

Blocking Passed Balls

Contributed by Jeff Mathis
DeMotte, Indiana

Full Team

Fielding

Base Running

Pitching

Hitting

Catching

Skill Focus

Builds confidence, develops footwork, and encourages dropping to the ground to block wild pitches.

Age Focus
9-12

Fun Rating

Fundamental Rating

Tennis balls are required for this drill, which encourages catchers to drop to the ground to smother wild pitches, a frightening prospect for many players. It can be nearly impossible to get youngsters to shift their weight quickly, open their hands, and go down to block pitches in the dirt.

☐ The Drill

Start with one of your catching position prospects in full gear, in front of the backstop. Before you begin throwing tennis balls, explain the purpose of the drill, which is to prevent wild pitches from getting past catchers.

The catcher will start in the normal catcher's crouch position, with feet even or slightly open to favor the throwing side. On wild pitches, the objective of the catcher is to do whatever it takes to prevent the ball from getting past him. This requires a basic instinct that is difficult to develop. However, it also requires several skills that can be developed.

Throw the first tennis ball from about 30 to 40 feet away, in the dirt, to either side of the catcher. Most inexperienced catchers will instinctively shy away from the ball, keeping their feet planted in their original spot and reaching half-heartedly to stop the ball only with the glove hand. Rarely will this action result in a successfully blocked ball.

Coaching Analysis

After this drill, the coach should analyze the following:

- Did the catcher start in the ready position (crouched) before each tennis ball was thrown?

- Did he move his feet quickly to get himself into "position" to block the ball?

- Did he block the ball with open hands?

- Did he drop to the ground, versus lifting up, to use his entire body as a blocking force?

Next, instruct the catcher to concentrate on moving his feet quickly to the right and then to the left, repeatedly, in rapid-fire succession, staying as low as possible in the process. After he gets the hang of moving his feet quickly, throw another ball, again aiming at the dirt on either side of him.

Next, teach the same foot movements, but add the open hands and dropping to the ground elements. On pitches in the dirt, both hands should be open, facing down, with palms toward the ball, and the player should drop to his knees to get his entire body prepared to block the pitch as necessary.

Throw several more pitches in the dirt to either side and directly in front of the catcher, offering instruction and encouragement between each pitch. Make sure he fields the pitch with open hands, dropping to the ground in order to use his entire body to prevent the ball from getting by him. Blocking the pitch successfully versus allowing it to go to the backstop will mean the difference in giving up a few stolen bases and giving up many stolen bases.

When the player is starting to wear out in this drill, move a little closer and throw eight or ten wild pitches in a row, rapid-fire, to finish the drill. If the player did anything well at all, give him lots of encouragement. Doing this in a game with real baseballs will be a long-term challenge, but this drill will give catchers the skills and confidence to meet that challenge.

Word Association Pitching

Contributed by Russ Thompson
Keene, New Hampshire

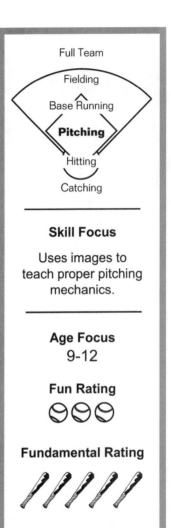

Full Team

Fielding

Base Running

Pitching

Hitting

Catching

Skill Focus

Uses images to teach proper pitching mechanics.

Age Focus
9-12

Fun Rating

Fundamental Rating

Sometimes 9- or 10-year-olds have difficulty remembering to go to the bathroom before the game, or what order they bat in the line up. Imagine a young pitcher trying to remember where his foot should be on the pitching rubber, not to open his hips too early, to hold the ball correctly, and five or six other things while trying to get the pitch near the plate. By giving the kids non-baseball images to picture, they'll find it easier to remember the primary mechanical elements of the pitching delivery. As they move up the ladder in organized baseball, they'll be able to fine-tune all these elements, but this drill will help lay the foundation.

❏ The Drill

The objective of this drill is to give kids fun images to help them remember the different steps in a pitching delivery. Have all of your pitching prospects stand behind you as you demonstrate each "image" of the delivery.

Diving Board

The first image is standing on a diving board. For instance, say to them, "You know how to stand on a diving board or on the side of the swimming pool. I want you to put your toes in the water." Then, facing away from each player, stand as though your feet are over the edge of the diving board. Make sure each player understands this image and repeats the motion of putting his toes over the front edge of the rubber.

Flamingo

The next image is imitating a flamingo. With your back still facing away from the pitchers, bring your glove up in front of you in a position that is comfortable (between the waist and the chin, depending on each player's comfort level)

with the pitching hand on the ball and inside the glove. Instruct the players to take a short step back about six inches with the lead leg (left leg for righties), and pivot on the throwing foot (right foot for righties), placing it in front of the rubber (not on top of the rubber). The lead leg then comes forward and up, imitating a flamingo. Instruct the players to hold this position for balance, as a flamingo would do, with the lead leg bent at the knee, as high as it can be comfortably held. Have each player hold this flamingo position as many as 25 times (without losing balance) before continuing to the next phase of the drill.

Conductor

The hips should now be facing third base (for righties), and the lead leg is ready to stride forward. The pitching hand

is still holding the ball inside the glove. Now, instruct each player to picture an orchestra conductor. What does a conductor do? He brings his hands out to the side, ready to move the batons to conduct the orchestra.

Instruct the players to imagine that they are the orchestra conductor, separating their hands so that the glove hand goes down and toward home plate and the throwing hand goes down and toward second base. As the hands separate and go down and back like an orchestra conductor, the hand should be holding the ball away from the pitcher's face, as though he is touching the ball on an imaginary wall toward second base.

As the arms separate, the lead foot should stride toward the plate as the pivot foot pushes off the front edge of the rubber with the knee bent slightly. Stop to draw a line in the dirt, straight from the rubber, about three or four feet toward the plate. This line will serve as a target for each player's lead foot. As the player pushes off, opens his arms, and strides toward the plate, landing near the target line with his lead foot, the hips open to allow the back leg to follow through.

<u>Release and Pick Up Grass</u>

The pitcher's eyes have been fixed on the target (usually the catcher's mitt) throughout each step of the delivery. As the lead foot plants near the target line, the throwing arm begins to whip forward in one continuous motion. The elbow leads and the wrist follows. In an overhand motion, the pitcher releases the ball with the snap of the wrist, aiming for the target as the baseball rolls off his fingertips. After the ball is released, the hips open (only after the release) and the right hip, leg, and foot follow the pitch toward the catcher, landing in a balanced defensive position. At this point, instruct the pitcher to "pick up grass," meaning to follow through far enough that the throwing hand can pick up imaginary grass off the ground.

Balance is critical. Throughout each step of the delivery – diving board, flamingo, orchestra conductor, stride forward, pitch release, and pick up grass – balance should be maintained.

Coaching Analysis

After this drill, the coach should analyze the following:

- **Did the pitchers stay balanced throughout each phase of the pitching delivery?**

- **Did they keep their eyes focused on the target?**

- **If any of them struggled with any particular phase of the delivery, have them work independently (with supervision) on the phase that presents the biggest challenge. Try not to correct too many deficiencies at one time. Focus on the most critical challenge for each particular player.**

Cutoff Relay Race

Contributed by Dennis Nickerson
Boulder, Colorado

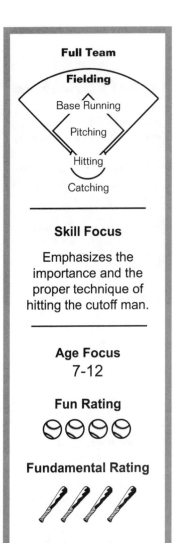

Full Team

Fielding
Base Running
Pitching
Hitting
Catching

Skill Focus

Emphasizes the importance and the proper technique of hitting the cutoff man.

Age Focus
7-12

Fun Rating

Fundamental Rating

When's the last time you saw a professional baseball player miss the cutoff man? It doesn't happen very often, does it? At the youth level, however, to say it happens frequently would be putting it mildly. Missing the cutoff man will give a coach ulcers more quickly than any other mistake in baseball. On the other hand, a great cutoff throw (at any level) can be a thing of beauty.

☐ The Drill

Divide your players into three groups of four or two groups of five to six players. Have them form straight lines, keeping at least 30 feet between each player for 7- to 8-year-olds, at least 40 feet for 9- to 10-year-olds, and at least 50 feet for 11- to 12-year-olds.

The player on one end of each line will begin the relay race by throwing a line drive to the next player in his line, the cutoff man, who will hold his arms up to give the thrower a target. Immediately after the thrower releases the ball, the cutoff man should turn his body sideways, so that his glove side is facing away from the thrower and toward the next cutoff man in line. He may have to move frontward or backwards, depending on the accuracy of the throw, in order to catch the ball and be in a position to quickly transfer the ball from the glove to the throwing hand and make a line drive throw to the next cutoff man in line.

Coaching Analysis

After this drill, the coach should analyze the following:

• Did the players raise their arms to provide a target for the throwers?

• Were the cutoff throws consistently near the cutoff man's head or chest?

• As each cutoff man prepared to catch the throw, did they turn sideways toward the next player targeted to receive the throw (that is, were they in a position to quickly make the next throw)?

• When the race was over, did all the players understand how cutoff throws and catches apply to game situations, and are they prepared to automatically make the appropriate cutoff throw and catch during a game?

When the ball reaches the end of the line, that player turns and throws back to the previous player. Each cutoff man (the player who's catching the cutoff throw) will give the thrower a target by raising his arms, and turning halfway toward the next cutoff man, catching the ball, and making the next throw. The first team to get the ball back to the beginning thrower wins the race.

After the race, explain to the players that all long throws from the outfield must be thrown to a cutoff man, and that the cutoff man in games should always run out to meet the cutoff throw, raise his arms to provide a target, turn with his glove side toward the next target, and make the throw that's appropriate for the play. This drill  should train the thrower and the cutoff man for game cutoff situations. After you've explained how this drill applies to game situations, run the race several more times. Cutoff throws can't be overdone.

Home Run Derby

Contributed by Bill Sandry
Bettendorf, Iowa

Full Team

Fielding

Base Running

Pitching

Hitting

Catching

Skill Focus

Teaches young players to swing hard; gives each player an opportunity for a moment of glory.

Age Focus
9-12

Fun Rating

Fundamental Rating

Who doesn't dream about hitting home runs? Even though most young players dream of such a feat, they often lack the confidence to swing hard enough to have a reasonable shot at hitting one. Conventional wisdom says young players should just "swing level" and "make contact," and the rest will take care of itself. Once players leave T-ball and begin playing coach pitch, hitting confidence can be hard to come by, even for skilled hitters. Kids who are struggling with confidence can overcome the problem in the Home Run Derby Drill. As Ted Williams said many years ago, "Swing hard just in case you hit something." This drill is fun, which is a big part of why kids play baseball.

☐ The Drill

Move home plate out to second base, facing the fence. If your practice field doesn't have a fence, try to find a soccer field or utility field that has a fence that could be safely adapted as a home run fence. Have your batting-practice pitching coach pitch to batters from shallow center field (about 40 feet away), at a slower speed than regular batting practice pitches. Have fielders spread out near the fence. Throw each batter ten or twelve slow pitches at a time, encouraging hard "home run swings." You may want to throw some "extra" pitches to the weaker hitters, giving them every opportunity to hit a dinger. Keep score. Give two points for each home run, and one point for each ball that hits the fence. For weaker hitters, modify the point system, giving

Coaching Analysis

After this drill, the coach should analyze the following:

- Did each player swing hard (that is, did the weaker players swing harder than they normally swing)?

- Did the players have fun? This drill should be a fun confidence booster for all!

points just for solid hits, or even for improved swings. Remember to make it fun for <u>all</u> the players.

As you can imagine, some players may develop severe undercut swings or accentuate the ones they already have. Try not to lose too much sleep over it. At this level, do anything you can to get players to swing the bat and build hitting confidence.

Backstop Toss

Contributed by Jon Gentile
New Castle, Delaware

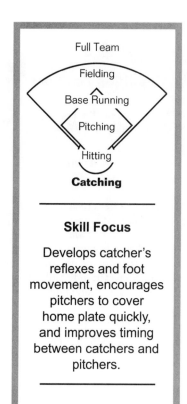

Skill Focus

Develops catcher's reflexes and foot movement, encourages pitchers to cover home plate quickly, and improves timing between catchers and pitchers.

Age Focus
9-12

Fun Rating

Fundamental Rating

Foot movement is critical in most sports and at most positions and levels in baseball. In Backstop Toss, quick foot movement is stressed at the pitcher and catcher positions. This drill only applies at kid-pitch levels where stealing home is allowed. For T-ballers and coach-pitchers, this drill will likely not apply.

Have a few base runners at third base and a few catchers behind the plate (one at a time for each). Have a few pitchers at the pitcher's mound, ready to cover home when the runner attempts to steal.

☐ The Drill

Instruct the catcher to get in the crouch position, as though he is awaiting a pitch. Instruct the runner on third to take a normal lead (not excessive), and the pitcher to be in the follow-through position at the mound. Stand behind the catcher, near the backstop, and drop a ball. Yell, "Go!," and move away from the ball. When the catcher hears "go", he should move immediately to find the ball, pick it up, turn, and toss it to the pitcher. The runner should immediately sprint toward home plate to score, and the pitcher should immediately sprint toward home (without first looking to see if the runner is going) to prevent the runner from scoring. There should be no hesitation by anyone. It is imperative that all three players go full speed in this drill,

Coaching Analysis

After this drill, the coach should analyze the following:

• Did the pitcher <u>not</u> look at the runner?

• Did catchers toss their helmets and masks after turning toward the backstop to run toward the ball (depending on your coaching strategy and the player's comfort level)?

• Did the catcher throw low and on the third base side of the plate?

• Did their throws beat the runners home?

• Did they slide to pick up the ball?

which assumes that a wild pitch or passed ball has gotten by the catcher while a runner is on third base.

Some coaches endorse getting rid of the helmet and mask after turning to chase after the ball. You may wish to experiment with the helmet and mask toss individually with each catcher.

With kneepads on, catchers shouldn't be tentative about sliding when they get close to the ball in order to pick it up quickly and aggressively. The toss to the pitcher should be low and toward the third base side of home plate so that a tag can be made easily on the sliding base runner. On most baseball diamonds, an underhand toss will be suitable, since the distance between the plate and the backstop won't likely be too great.

Again, have all three players assume their respective ready positions. Then drop another ball in a different place near the back stop, and yell "go". Again, the catcher should sprint toward the ball, go down to get it, and toss it to the pitcher, who again should tag the runner. Make sure the pitcher doesn't hesitate by looking to see if the runner is going. He should assume that every runner at third base is stealing on any wild pitch or passed ball. Once he has started to sprint home, it's okay to quickly glance to see if the runner has committed.

Run this drill over and over at full speed, making sure none of the three players hesitates.

4 on 4 on 4

Contributed by Rob Cruz
Ellicott City, Maryland

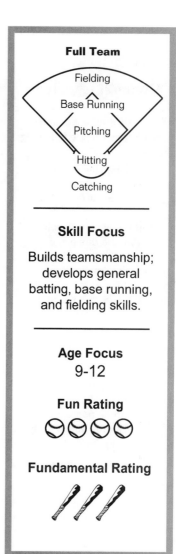

Full Team

Fielding
Base Running
Pitching
Hitting
Catching

Skill Focus

Builds teamsmanship; develops general batting, base running, and fielding skills.

Age Focus
9-12

Fun Rating

Fundamental Rating

Drills can be great tools for developing specific mechanical or fundamental skills for individual players. The 4 on 4 on 4 drill is really more of an abbreviated and accelerated game, without targeted skill development, but with specific benefits that traditional drills don't necessarily provide. The 4 on 4 on 4 drill offers accelerated batting, base running, and fielding practice in a game-like atmosphere. During this drill, defensive players should be encouraged to be smart and conservative, while batters and base runners may elect to be more aggressive than they usually are.

☐ The Drill

Divide players into teams of four each. Make every attempt to split the teams evenly, according to skill level, position preference, and experience level. Send one team to the infield positions (3B, SS, 2B, 1B). Send another team to the outfield positions (LF, CF, and RF, with the remaining player covering the pitcher's position as the coach pitches). Send the remaining team to the dugout to hit. The coach (or parent) who throws the most accurate batting practice pitches should pitch for this drill. You want every player swinging at as many good pitches as possible. Have a parent play the catcher's position from the backstop. Stealing is not permitted.

The batting team has two complete "innings" in which to hit, under game-like conditions. With all fielding players

Coaching Analysis

After this drill, the coach should analyze the following:

- Did defensive players play in a smart and conservative manner?

- Did the players hustle during the game <u>and</u> during the transitions between innings?

- Did the hitters swing and run the bases aggressively?

- Were any players overly challenged when quizzed about situations? If so, those specific concerns need to be addressed one-on-one immediately following the drill.

in the ready position, the player in the pitching position stands next to the coach, who pitches to the batting team. Other coaches or parents coach first base and third base, giving appropriate signals and coaching advice as players reach their base, and giving kids the sense that they are in a real game. The pitcher (coach) calls balls and strikes, and the hitting team is allowed three outs. Again, the coach pitches to each batter from the hitting team, keeping track of the pitch count and the number of outs. Encourage batters to swing freely. At this age, swinging at a pitch over the batter's head is more beneficial than standing and looking at a third strike.

This is an ideal time for coaches to focus on defensive thinking. Every once in a while, turn to one of the infield or outfield players and ask him what he's going to do if the ball comes to him in this situation. For instance, with nobody out and runners on first and second, you might ask your third baseman what he will do if the next batter hits a grounder to him.

When the hitting team has gotten all three outs for the second time, the infield team hustles in to hit. The hitting team hustles to the outfield and the outfield team hustles to the infield. This drill allows each player to play at least two or three positions defensively, and wears players out from extensive hitting and base running.

If only nine or ten players show up at practice, you might modify the drill to be 4 on 4, with parents filling in the outfield positions. This may be a good time to have one or two pitchers or catchers working with a coach on individual skills away from the field.

Pitcher Covering First Base

Contributed by Mike Miselis
Bayonne, New Jersey

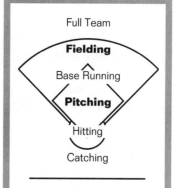

Full Team

Fielding

Base Running

Pitching

Hitting

Catching

Skill Focus

Improves communication between pitcher, first baseman, and second baseman; creates a mindset in the pitcher to automatically run toward first base on all ground balls to the right side of the infield.

Age Focus
9-12

Fun Rating

Fundamental Rating

Even at the major league level, you'll occasionally witness a mental lapse by a pitcher, and consequently a base runner that should have been an easy out had the pitcher remembered to cover first base. This drill will help pitchers practice this essential skill and hopefully make their move to cover first base second nature.

☐ The Drill

Start with all your pitching prospects, two or three first base prospects, a catcher, and a second baseman. Explain to each player in the drill the importance of covering first base on ground balls to the right side of the infield. Then have everybody get into ready position. Stand at first base and have the pitcher throw to the catcher. After the catcher fields the pitch, he throws a medium-speed grounder between the first baseman and the second baseman. Ideally, this grounder should make the first baseman field the ball.

Immediately upon impact, all three players (not including the catcher) will move toward the ball. The first baseman must judge whether to continue moving to field the ball or to go back to first base and let the ball go through to the second baseman. For the purposes of the drill, which is

Coaching Analysis

After this drill, the coach should analyze the following:

• Did each first baseman make the proper judgment to field the ball or allow it to go through to the second baseman?

• Did the pitcher immediately break toward first base each time the catcher threw a grounder? This is the key to this drill.

• Were the tosses from the first baseman to the pitcher chest-high, and did they "lead" the pitcher soon enough for the pitcher to catch the toss before reaching the base?

• Did the pitcher step on the inside corner of first base?

primarily for the benefit of pitchers, you'd like to have the first baseman field most of the grounders.

As the first baseman is moving to field the ball, the pitcher is running toward first base, ready to take a toss from the first baseman. When the first baseman has successfully fielded the baseball, he must judge whether to run to first base to beat the base runner himself or to toss the ball underhanded to the pitcher, who should be able to beat the base runner to the base.

There are times in baseball when a throw should be at a base, whether the player who is to receive the throw is at the base or not. This is not one of those times. When the first baseman fields the grounder and determines that he is going to toss the ball to the pitcher, he must do so quickly, "leading" the pitcher slightly. The toss should be chest high and should give the pitcher time to field the ball a few steps ahead of getting to the base in order to avoid a possible collision with the base runner.

As the pitcher reaches first base, he should attempt to step on the corner of the base closest to the pitcher's mound, then finish running toward right field, not across the baseline in the path of the runner. When the play is over, offer any praise or instruction, then have the next pitcher and the next first baseman take their ready positions, along with the catcher and the second baseman. Again, the pitcher will pitch the ball, and the catcher will throw a grounder between the first baseman and the second baseman.

Occasionally instruct the catcher to mix the speed and direction of the grounders, so that the pitchers and the second baseman will have to field some balls.

Point & Pull Long Toss

Contributed by Dennis Nickerson
Boulder, Colorado

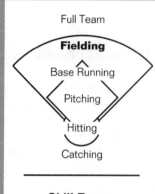

Full Team

Fielding

Base Running

Pitching

Hitting

Catching

Skill Focus

Develops throwing
mechanics, warms
up the body and the
throwing arm, and
develops throwing arm
strength.

Age Focus
9-12

Fun Rating

Fundamental Rating

Before every practice and every game, players should do some stretching and throwing. After stretching, always have the players throw in pairs in two lines (at least 30 feet apart for 9- to 10-year-olds, and 40 to 50 feet apart for 11- to 12-year-olds). Even warm-ups should be organized to promote teamsmanship and prevent injuries. There should be at least ten feet between players in the same line (next to each other, not across from each other). Once they're warmed up (at least 25 throws each), begin the Point & Pull Long Toss Drill.

☐ The Drill

Have each player back up one step, point his glove at the target (the head of the player he is throwing to), reach back with his throwing hand (fingers on top, pointing the baseball toward an imaginary wall behind him), arch his back slightly, step toward the target with the lead leg (for a right-handed thrower, this would be the left leg), pull his glove back to his chest, and throw across his body in an overhand motion toward the target.

The thrower then steps back to receive a throw from the other player, who goes through the same throwing mechanics. This process continues, with each player retreating one step after throwing the ball. Remember, even at longer distances, the goal of the throw is still to reach the target player in line drive form. As the players continue to

Coaching Analysis

After this drill, the coach should analyze the following:

- Did players use proper throwing mechanics in the warm-up portion of the drill?

- Did players use proper throwing mechanics in the long-toss portion of the drill?

- Did they point their gloves toward the target before each throw?

- Were the throws still in nearly line-drive form, even as the distance to the target increased?

back up one step after each throw, the throws will naturally become slightly arched as the distance between the two players increases. This is okay to a point. Once the throws get to a distance that is too great to reach the target in nearly line drive form, each player should change the target from the head to the knee of the opposite player. In fact, a strong line drive throw that bounces once before being caught at the knees is still an ideal throw.

This drill will strengthen young players' arms and help them focus on hitting a long-range target. Outfield throws to cutoff players and base targets will be improved by this drill. Be careful not to wear out young players' arms with too many long throws.

Water Sliding

Contributed by Gilbert Lopez
Round Rock, Texas

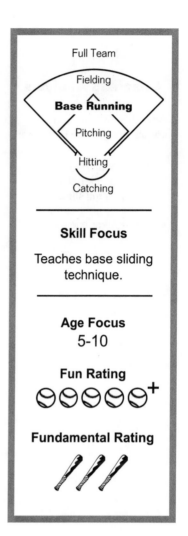

Skill Focus

Teaches base sliding technique.

Age Focus
5-10

Fun Rating

Fundamental Rating

Teaching young kids how to slide into third base is easier said than done. Ever try to slide on dirt and small rocks as an adult? It doesn't always feel pleasant, does it? From age five to about age eight, sliding is often not allowed in community leagues, for obvious safety reasons. Where it is allowed, and for 9- to 12-year-olds, use something that makes learning to slide much more fun -- a water slide.

They can be found at any toy store for twenty to thirty dollars. There's a good chance someone on the team already has one, and would be willing to share. You don't even necessarily have to have a hose and a water source. The next time you're thinking of canceling practice because of rain, tell the kids to bring their swimsuits instead (provided, of course, that there is no threat of lightning).

☐ The Drill

Find a level area. Check the ground for rocks, ruts, and so on. Then lay down the vinyl sliding mat. Concentrate only on feet-first slides (most leagues have outlawed headfirst sliding). The coach demonstrates the proper sliding position by lying down on his backside. Slightly favoring one side (say, your right side), put your right leg under your left, bent at the knee, in a figure-4 shape. Make fists with both hands, and put most of your weight on your right thigh, hip and buttock area, where most of the energy of the slide will be absorbed. Have the players look carefully at

Coaching Analysis

After this drill, the coach should analyze the following:

- Did the player run fast enough to carry him through a full slide?

- Did he favor one side?

- Was he in a figure-4 position?

- Was his upper body low toward the ground?

- Were his fists closed?

this position while you are laying still. Then, take a running start and do the same thing while sliding onto the water slide, holding the prone, figure-4 position throughout the slide. The head and shoulders should be low toward the ground, not sitting upright.

One at a time, the players take running starts and slide on the water slide, attempting to copy the position the coach has demonstrated. Make sure the players get long, running starts. Once they start sliding on dirt, it's a whole lot easier to actually "slide" if they are running fast (and it hurts less). The players should gradually go into the slide, versus jumping in the air and dropping to the ground quickly, which is more dangerous (and hurts more). The figure-4 will help them slide to a side, where  their bodies can best absorb the slide. The closed fists will keep young players from trying to brace themselves once they start sliding on dirt, helping to prevent hand and wrist injuries.

Bombard the Facemask

Contributed by Russ Thompson
Keene, New Hampshire

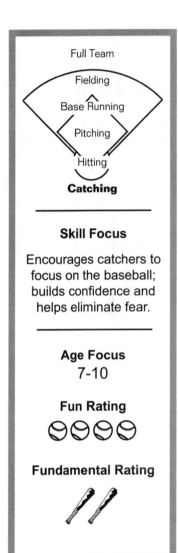

Full Team

Fielding

Base Running

Pitching

Hitting

Catching

Skill Focus

Encourages catchers to focus on the baseball; builds confidence and helps eliminate fear.

Age Focus
7-10

Fun Rating

Fundamental Rating

At most levels of play, the catcher position is a critical position in which few players show signs of interest.

At the youth level, however, the catcher position can have mass appeal. Kids think it's cool to wear all that equipment, and some will beg to give it a try. Others will be scared to death of it, and may not possess the eye-hand coordination to play the position well. Even for the kids who can't wait to give it a try, and possess the necessary skills, this drill is effective at building confidence, eliminating fear, and teaching the importance of focus at the catcher position.

☐ The Drill

Keep some "reduced injury factor" (soft) baseballs handy, along with some tennis balls. Have catchers wear the full catcher's gear, except the catcher's mitt, and stand a few feet in front of the backstop. Instruct the players to assume the ready position, which will instinctively cause them to mentally prepare for the next part of the drill.

Next, let the players know that you are going to throw balls at their facemask, and that they should attempt to keep from blinking throughout the drill. Start with the tennis balls, and stand just a few feet away, throwing softly at the player's mask. When the player blinks as the first ball hits the mask (and he probably will), encourage him to focus a little harder, and throw another tennis ball directly at the

Coaching Analysis

After this drill, the coach should analyze the following:

- Did the players stand in the ready position, prepared for action?

- Were the players able to stay focused enough to keep from blinking when the baseballs hit their facemask?

mask. After ten or fifteen throws, make the throws a few inches to the side , and instruct the player to move his head to block the ball with the facemask, again trying not to blink.

For older, more confident catchers, change to "reduced injury factor" baseballs. Again, stand a few feet away and bombard the player's facemask, one ball at a time, noticing if he is able to keep his eyes open throughout the drill. A catcher has a lot to focus on during a game. If he is able to focus during the drill, chances are he will be able to focus during the game.

Swing 'Til You Miss

Contributed by Jay Hinson
Cheraw, South Carolina

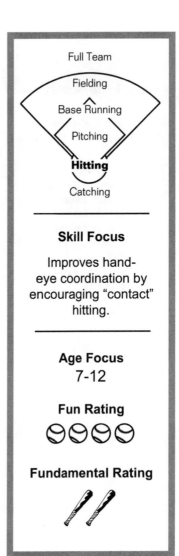

Full Team

Fielding

Base Running

Pitching

Hitting

Catching

Skill Focus

Improves hand-eye coordination by encouraging "contact" hitting.

Age Focus
7-12

Fun Rating

Fundamental Rating

Here's a drill that's like a billiards game or a foul-shooting contest. As long as you continue making shots, you get to keep shooting. In this case, as long as you make contact with each swing, you get to keep swinging.

☐ The Drill

While other drills are going on in other areas of the practice field, pitch to one batter at a time, with parents or other players handling the infield positions. The object of the drill is to make contact with the ball on each and every swing. It doesn't matter if it's fair or foul. As long as each hitter makes any kind of contact, they stay in the batter's box and continue batting.

Instruct each batter to adjust his swing as though it's the bottom of the sixth, there are two outs, the bases are loaded, and he's up to bat. Instruct the batters to choke up an inch or two on the bat, shorten their stride toward the pitcher, and make a compact swing at any close pitch. By making these three swing modifications, players will increase their chances of making contact.

If the hitter lets a strike go by, he's out. If he swings and completely misses the pitch, he's out. If he lets the pitch go, and it's a ball, he keeps hitting. If he swings and makes any kind of contact whatsoever, fair or foul, he keeps hitting.

Coaching Analysis

After this drill, the coach should analyze the following:

- Did each player make the necessary swing adjustments to become a "contact" hitter:
  - Shorter stride?
  - Choked up on the bat?
  - More compact swing rotation?

Make this drill into a contest. For two consecutive hits (contacts), maybe give out one piece of bubble gum. For five hits, maybe a candy bar would be appropriate at your team's level. You may even wish to keep track throughout the season. Perhaps two free video rentals could be given to the player with the highest number of consecutive hits at the end of the year. How about the most improved contact hitter? Without publicizing the award, maybe the player who improves the most dramatically (goes from one consecutive hit to seven, for instance) from the first practice to the last practice could win a baseball movie video. Be creative!

Zig-Zag

Contributed by Gilbert Lopez
Round Rock, Texas

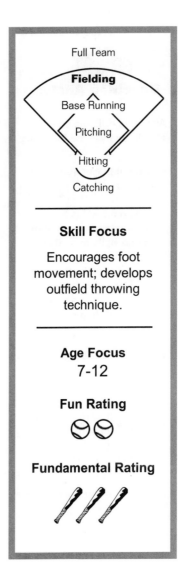

Full Team

Fielding

Base Running

Pitching

Hitting

Catching

Skill Focus

Encourages foot
movement; develops
outfield throwing
technique.

Age Focus
7-12

Fun Rating

Fundamental Rating

Let's face it, the outfield can be a lonely place sometimes. There's not always a lot of action out there. From T-ball through the 9-10 age division, many coaches prefer to put their "sand angels" in the outfield where they aren't likely to get hurt. Sand angels are players who lack the interest level or attention span to focus on the game. They tend to play in the dirt and look around in all directions but the batter's box. Coaches generally need to accept the reality that younger sand angels are just part of youth baseball, and that they aren't at risk from many line drives from 7- or 8-year-olds.

By the age of 11 or 12 (and experienced 9- or 10-year-olds), where some kids are capable of hitting the ball with significant power, outfielders need to be encouraged to stay focused and interested, and not become too complacent. The zig-zag drill gets outfielders used to moving their feet to get to the ball in order to make strong throws to the infielders in the cutoff positions or directly to the bases. If outfielders (at any level) feel excited about getting to the ball quickly and making an effective throw, they will tend to stay more focused.

☐ The Drill

Line up five or six players at the fence (or about 100 feet behind second base if there is no fence). Have a coach straddle second base, and another play cutoff man. Prior to

Coaching Analysis

After this drill, the coach should analyze the following:

- **Did the player start in the ready position?**

- **Did he move his feet quickly to get to each of the six balls to be thrown?**

- **Did he rush the throws once he made the pick-up, or did he make a controlled hop-step as he threw?**

- **Were his throws hard "line drives" at the head of the cutoff man?**

- **Did the players find their target (the cutoff man) on the zig-zag balls while moving away from the infield?**

starting the drill, place six baseballs on the ground in two lines, starting about 20 feet from the players, with the balls about ten feet apart in a zig-zag position.

The first player starts in the ready position. The coach says, "go", and the player sprints to the closest ball, grabs it with his throwing hand, takes a quick hop-step toward the cutoff man, and throws a hard line drive throw to the head of the cutoff man, who is waving both hands to provide a target. The coach (cutoff man) catches the throw and throws to the second baseman, as if it is a game situation.

The player immediately runs to the next closest ball in the zig-zag formation, grabs it and again takes a hop-step and throws to the head of the cutoff man.

The player continues the zig-zag drill until all six balls have been picked up and thrown to the cutoff man. Each of the six throws will be closer to the infield, so the cutoff man should back up a few feet with each throw, judging the arm strength of the thrower in the process, and moving closer or further away from the thrower accordingly. Strongly encourage each player to make hard, line drive throws to the head of the cutoff man, regardless of the player's talent level.

Praise quick foot movement by players, along with accurate cutoff throws. Many positive things are possible with quick foot movement.

Once players have mastered the zig-zag, reverse the direction and go backward, away from second base. Have them start at the ball that's closest to the infield, turn and throw to the cutoff man, then go to the next baseballs, one at a time, moving away from the infield. As the player moves further away, the cutoff man needs to move out toward him and provide a target.

Simon Says

Contributed by Jon Brainard
San Dimas, California

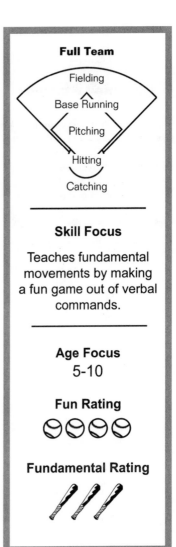

Full Team

Fielding
Base Running
Pitching
Hitting
Catching

Skill Focus

Teaches fundamental movements by making a fun game out of verbal commands.

Age Focus
5-10

Fun Rating

Fundamental Rating

With young athletes, repetition and reinforcement are critical elements of learning sports fundamentals. "Old school" baseball coaches believe in hitting a thousand grounders to a player and offering repetitive verbal instruction to teach the fundamentals of handling those grounders. Try this drill as an alternative to the "old school" method of repetitive instruction by teaching movements without including actual baseball playing.

☐ The Drill

Line up all the players in three or four rows, all facing you while you lead a game of Simon Says. Instead of the

standard game instructions, hold a baseball up and yell baseball movements such as "Simon says, shuffle step left," as you move the baseball in the direction the players are to move. Then  yell "Simon says, cross-over step right," or "Simon says ready position," or another baseball related movement. Occasionally, offer an instruction without saying "Simon

Coaching Analysis

After this drill, the coach should analyze the following:

- Did the players learn some of the basic movements and have fun?

says," and have other coaches or parents help to catch players who move erroneously. Players who make the wrong movement or move when Simon didn't say to move are out.

Every once in a while, say left, but move the ball right. The kids will get a kick out of this. Offer a nice prize to the last player standing.

Some possible movements for Simon Says could include:

- Ready position
- Sacrifice bunt
- Crow hop (hop-step)
- Gorilla grounder
- Level swing
- Shuffle step (right, left)
- Cross-over step (right, left, front, back)
- Alligator
- Pop-up catch
- Flamingo
- Charge grounder
- Any other baseball movements you can create

One & Gun

Contributed by Ryan Callaham
Round Rock, Texas

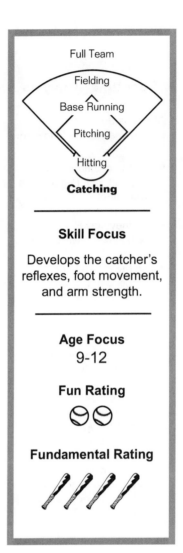

Full Team

Fielding

Base Running

Pitching

Hitting

Catching

Skill Focus

Develops the catcher's reflexes, foot movement, and arm strength.

Age Focus
9-12

Fun Rating

Fundamental Rating

Throughout most levels of baseball, the catcher position is often the most challenging. It can be very difficult to find a player who has the enthusiasm, fearlessness, and the appropriate skill set for this challenging position. As players get experience at the catcher position, their skills and enthusiasm can improve. This drill will help with those things, but it will be instrumental in addressing the fearlessness issue. Make sure each catcher who participates in this drill is wearing proper protective gear, including a cup.

☐ The Drill

Take a bucket of baseballs (20 or so) to the pitcher's mound, and have players at third base, shortstop, second base, first base, and catcher. With players in the ready position, pitch one ball in the dirt in front of the catcher, and yell the name of a base, such as "third." The catcher should move his feet quickly to get in front of the pitch in the dirt, block it (with the catcher's mitt open and low), pick it up, take a hop-step toward the target base, and throw a line drive to the base you called. (In later years, the hop-step will be replaced by a quick release.) The players at each position move immediately to cover each base, catching the throw and tagging an imaginary base stealer. Even if the throw is to third base, all other infielders should move to cover a base or back up another player. Players should never

Coaching Analysis

After this drill, the coach should analyze the following:

- Did the catchers move their feet well to get to the errant pitch?

- Did they stay low to block the ball with their body?

- Did they keep their catcher's mitt open and pointing toward the ground?

- Did they take a hop-step toward the target base before throwing the ball?

- Did they make strong line drive throws to the fielders at each base?

- Did the other infielders stay involved, moving their feet to take a throw at the base, or to back up another player?

stand flat-footed. They should be taught to move their feet constantly.

Pitch the next ball in the dirt and yell another base, perhaps "second". Again, the catcher moves quickly to knock the ball down, picks it up, takes a hop-step, and fires to the target base. The second baseman puts the tag on an imaginary runner.

Continue to throw pitches in the dirt near the catcher, occasionally firing a strike to keep the catcher from moving too early from his ready position. After 20 pitches or so, switch to your next catcher, and repeat the drill.

As your catchers improve at blocking pitches, introduce base runners to the format, having one or two runners steal only after the catcher touches the ball. This will be good practice for the runners, as well. Be careful not to force each catcher to make too many throws. Twenty strong throws by each catcher should be plenty.

Leading Off & Stealing

Contributed by JC Petersen
Okemos, Michigan

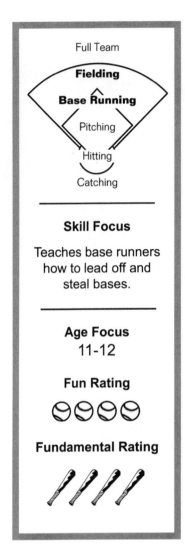

Full Team

Fielding

Base Running

Pitching

Hitting

Catching

Skill Focus

Teaches base runners
how to lead off and
steal bases.

Age Focus
11-12

Fun Rating

Fundamental Rating

In leagues where leading off and base stealing are permitted, it is important that kids become comfortable, if not accomplished, in this challenging area. Skilled base runners can change the entire complexion of a game.

☐ The Drill

Select a few players to be base runners, along with a first baseman, a catcher, a shortstop and a second baseman. Stand on the pitcher's mound and instruct the first-base runner to prepare to take a lead, focusing his eyes on you, the pitcher. Have the first baseman face the pitcher, with his right foot against the edge of the base that's closest to home plate, holding his glove out to provide a target for the pitcher (in this case, you). Have a parent or player serve as first-base coach to yell for the base runner to get back to base if the pitcher attempts a pickoff throw.

Once the pitcher gets into position on the rubber, instruct the runner to begin taking his lead, stepping sideways one step at a time. It is important that players not cross one foot in front of the other as they lead off the base. Instead, they should shuffle sideways a foot at a time, with eyes trained on the pitcher, until they get just far enough that they can safely get back to the base if you attempt to pick them off.

Next, tell the runner to get into a ready position, with his feet spread wider than shoulder-width apart, and to prepare to make a decision based on the pitcher's action. If the pitcher tries to pick off the runner, he should break back to the base before the throw reaches the first baseman. Once the runner touches the base, he should stay on the base and turn to make sure the first baseman has thrown the ball back to the pitcher. Then, as the pitcher makes contact with the rubber to prepare for the next pitch, the runner should take his lead, again keeping his eyes on the pitcher.

Pitch the next one to the catcher, and instruct the runner to break for second base as soon as he recognizes that the pitcher is starting his pitching motion. The runner should automatically slide when he reaches second base, as the throw arrives from the catcher to the shortstop, with the second baseman backing up the throw.

Encourage kids to be aggressive when they lead off, taking an extra step until they get picked off. It's better to get picked off in practice, and subsequently learn individual limitations, than to be uncertain in practice and get picked off in the game. For players who have the ability to dive back into the base headfirst, encourage them to dive away from the fielder and toward the right field side of the base. Also, teach them to call time out after safely diving back to the base to avoid a trick tag-out by the first baseman.

After players have had several opportunities to lead off first base and steal second, instruct them to move to second base. Again, as the pitcher, take your position on the rubber and advise the runner to lead off, this time taking a bigger lead than at first base, since fielders won't generally hold the runner on at second. Runners do, however, need to keep an eye out for the shortstop sneaking around behind them for a quick pickoff throw from the pitcher. Again, the first base coach should be there to yell if the runner needs to get back to the base.

Moving to third base, runners should take their leads more conservatively, and in foul territory. The third baseman will be able to play close to the base, forcing the runner to stay fairly close to the base, too. When taking a lead at third, the runner needs to keep his eyes on the pitcher. Once the pitcher has made a move toward home plate, the runner at third should quickly run several steps toward home plate, in case a passed ball or wild pitch presents an opportunity to steal home. The same is true at first or second, but remind runners to be prepared to get back to the base quickly after the catcher handles the pitch.

Occasionally instruct runners to steal the next base, reminding them to slide properly. The more leading, stealing, and sliding they do in practice, the better they'll be in games.

Coaching Analysis

After this drill, the coach should analyze the following:

- Did the runners step sideways to get their leads, versus crossing one foot over the other?

- Did runners keep their eyes focused on you, the pitcher?

- Did you keep each runner guessing? Did you throw home on some throws and attempt to pick off some runners? Make it easy on them at first, but do some quick pick-off moves once the runners have the hang of it. You should see bigger leads at the next game.

- Did runners move forward several steps as the pitcher threw home?

- Did runners take their leads in foul territory at third base?

- Did runners successfully steal a few bases and gain confidence for attempting steals in games?

Pickle

Contributed by JC Petersen
Okemos, Michigan

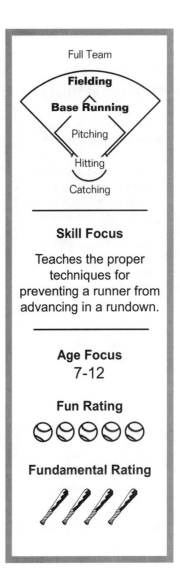

Full Team

Fielding

Base Running

Pitching

Hitting

Catching

Skill Focus

Teaches the proper techniques for preventing a runner from advancing in a rundown.

Age Focus
7-12

Fun Rating

Fundamental Rating

Pickle is a lot of fun, but it's one of the most difficult defensive skills to properly execute. In youth baseball, very few rundowns prevent the runner from advancing to the next base or further. Pickle is a prevention drill. The object for the defensive players is to prevent the runner who's caught between bases from reaching the lead base.

☐ **The Drill**

Set up two stations for the pickle rundown drill, one between first and second bases, and one between third and home. Start out by having an experienced coach serve as the runner who is caught in the "pickle," and have four players on defense at each station.

Before you begin the pickle drill, demonstrate the proper technique for preventing the runner from advancing to the next base:

Step 1 – When you spot a runner who is caught between bases, yell "pickle," so that your teammates are aware that there is a rundown situation.

Step 2 – The infielder with the ball should immediately run directly toward the runner, making the runner commit toward one base.

Step 3 – If the runner moves ahead toward the next base (toward second base if he's between first and second),

Coaching Analysis

After this drill, the coach should analyze the following:

• Did the fielder with the ball run directly toward the base runner, forcing him to commit to one base?

• Did the fielder with the ball hold it in a cocked arm position while running the base runner back towards the previous base?

• Did other fielders rotate into position to protect the base, placing themselves between the runner and the base to take a throw?

• Was the outcome of pickle either:
  - an out, or
  - a safe call at the previous base (versus the next base)?

immediately throw the ball to the fielder who's between second base and the runner.

Step 4 – If the fielder can make the tag, obviously the tag should be made. If not, the fielder with the ball should run toward the base runner, chasing him back to the previous base. The fielder should hold the ball with his arm cocked back the whole way, ready to make a throw if necessary at the last possible moment.

Step 5 – If the runner makes it back almost to the base, a throw should be made to the fielder who is between the base and the runner, who will apply the tag to the runner just as the runner is attempting to get safely back to that base.

Step 6 – If the tag is not applied, and the runner changes direction to go toward the lead base, a quick throw should be made to the other fielder, who has rotated in to protect the lead base.

Step 7 – Again, the fielder should run the base runner all the way back to the previous base, holding the ball with the arm cocked back, ready to make a last-minute throw as the runner attempts to get safely back to the base.

The idea is to make as few throws as possible, and to end up with the base runner either being tagged out or called safe at the previous base. If the runner makes it back safely to the base, teach the players to call time out immediately. Remind the kids not to fake throws during a rundown. It only creates a delay in re-cocking the arm, and it chases back the fielder more than it fakes out the runner.

Keep in mind that if a pickle ensues in a situation in which there are two or three base runners, always teach players to concentrate on the lead runner. Runners should never advance in a pickle. The ideal outcome is an out on the lead runner or all runners safe at the previous bases.

Two-Tee Batting

Contributed by Ryan Callaham
Round Rock, Texas

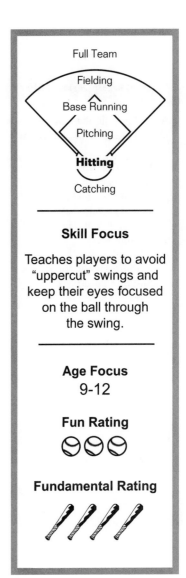

Full Team

Fielding

Base Running

Pitching

Hitting

Catching

Skill Focus

Teaches players to avoid "uppercut" swings and keep their eyes focused on the ball through the swing.

Age Focus
9-12

Fun Rating

Fundamental Rating

Many young players automatically develop uppercut swings when they are learning to hit a baseball. Fly balls just look cooler than ground balls. When they show highlights on TV, they don't show many grounders. They usually show home runs, which adds to a young player's desire to "uppercut" in an attempt to hit the long ball. Home runs are great, but a young player who consistently hits line drives and hard grounders is far more likely to make it as a hitter than a player who swings for the fences at a young age.

☐ The Drill

Instead of having hitters swing at a ball on a tee, line up two tees, front to back. The front tee is in the batter's normal swing path. Place a ball on the tee at a height that is comfortable for that particular hitter. Now, place a second tee just behind the first tee so that the base of each tee is touching each other. Next, place a ball on the second tee, slightly higher (a half-inch to an inch) than the ball on the front tee.

Each batter takes his normal stance at the front tee. As he swings, his bat must swing over the ball on the back tee in order to hit the ball on the front tee. This forces the hitter to swing in a downward motion, rather than an uppercut motion. It also forces players to keep their eyes fixed on the target ball through the entire swing. Level swings and

Coaching Analysis

After this drill, the coach should analyze the following:

- Did hitters swing in a downward motion, avoiding the ball on the back tee while making contact with the ball on the front tee?

- Did hitters keep their eyes fixed on the target ball through the entire swing?

- Did they make consistent contact, hitting line drives and hard grounders?

downward swings ultimately produce more successful hitters.

Offer praise for hard grounders hit during this drill. Hard grounders are always preferable to pop-ups, and Two-Tee Batting should net very positive results in this area.

Throwing Out Base Stealers

Contributed by Richard Nagata
Aiea, Hawaii

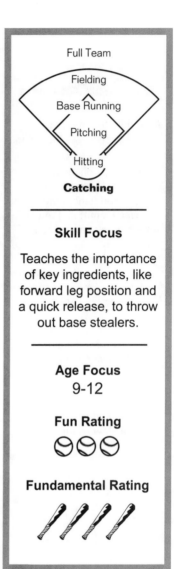

Full Team
Fielding
Base Running
Pitching
Hitting
Catching

Skill Focus

Teaches the importance of key ingredients, like forward leg position and a quick release, to throw out base stealers.

Age Focus
9-12

Fun Rating

Fundamental Rating

Don't be fooled into thinking that catchers must have cannons for arms. An enthusiastic catcher with a good glove, an average arm, and a quick release can be very effective at throwing out base stealers.

☐ The Drill

There are a few keys to teaching young catchers to throw out runners:

1. Hand Position – line up your catchers and have them assume their catcher's stance, with head up, back straight, feet slightly apart, and glove hand just behind the catcher's mitt, resting on it slightly. By positioning the throwing hand just behind the mitt, it will be protected from foul tips, and it will be in a position to quickly grab the ball to throw out the runner.

2. Leg Position – as the catchers are crouched with runner(s) on base, instruct them to spread their feet slightly further, moving the right foot back about six inches, and point the throwing knee (right knee for right-handed throwers) out toward the first baseman. This position prepares the catcher to pop back quickly to the right foot and just release the ball.

3. Ball Transfer – when the pitch hits the catcher's mitt, the catcher's throwing hand is already in position

Coaching Analysis

After this drill, the coach should analyze the following:

- Did the catchers each keep their throwing hands protected behind their catcher's mitt and ready for a quick ball exchange?

- Did they assume a crouched position with the glove leg forward and the throwing leg back?

- Did they transfer the ball quickly from the mitt to the throwing hand?

- Did they release the ball quickly with a low throw, versus taking a full step and a slow windup?

(behind the mitt) to grab the ball quickly to make the throw. This is a skill that young players can practice on their own at any time.

4. Quick Release – At this level, a player running from first base to second base can make it in about four seconds or so, which translates to two feet of running for every one-tenth of a second. Tell your catchers that a half-second delay in getting the ball to the lead base equals about ten feet of running by the base stealer. A quick ball exchange and release can dramatically improve the chance of throwing out the runner. Instead of taking a hop-step and full windup, teach your catchers to pop back quickly on the back foot (which is already back slightly) and release the ball quickly in an overhand motion toward the base

the runner is trying to steal. Even a low throw that bounces once or twice can be much more effective if delivered quickly than a rifle throw that results from a poor ball exchange and a slow, full windup.

By combining the proper hand position, leg position, ball transfer, and quick release, your catchers can improve their chances of throwing out base stealers. Remember to encourage low throws, even if they bounce to the target base.

Once your catching prospects have been schooled on the key elements of throwing out base stealers, put a runner on first base and have him attempt to steal second base, as the catcher combines these elements to throw him out. Then, have another runner try to steal second. Next, try some attempted steals at third base. Remember not to wear out the catchers' arms with too many throws.

4-Square

Contributed by Ryan Callaham
Round Rock, Texas

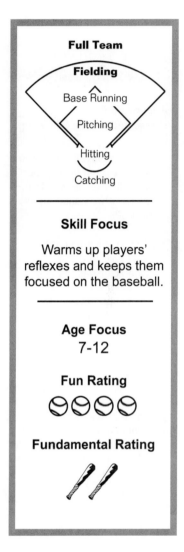

Full Team

Fielding
Base Running
Pitching
Hitting
Catching

Skill Focus

Warms up players' reflexes and keeps them focused on the baseball.

Age Focus
7-12

Fun Rating

Fundamental Rating

This drill works well with four players or an entire team. It's sort of a "hot potato" for baseball. It works as a warm-up drill or a competitive game for the entire team.

☐ The Drill

Put four players in a square formation, about 20-40 feet apart, depending on the ages and reflexive skills. Initially, try to match kids evenly for skill level. Later, in the full-team version of 4-Square, mix up the talent level to make the teams even.

With the players in a square, in the ready position, throw a ball to one of them, and instruct him to catch it and immediately throw it to another player in the square. That player will then throw the ball quickly to a different member of the square. Staying in the ready position, each player prepares to catch a quick throw and immediately make a quick throw to a different player. Because the throws can come closely and quickly from any direction, each player must keep incredibly focused and ready for action.

For players who are skilled enough for a more competitive version of 4-Square turn the drill into a full team "hot potato," with two or three teams of four players for each square. Have each team count out loud how many successful catches they make in 30 seconds. If any member

Coaching Analysis

After this drill, the coach should analyze the following:

- Did each player stay in the ready position throughout the drill or game, staying completely focused on all throws?

- Did all the participants stay interested and involved? Keep in mind that the stronger players may avoid throwing to weaker players. Use your judgment. If the weaker players can safely participate, make sure they are involved in the drill. If necessary, modify the rules to keep all players actively participating.

of a team drops one of the throws, that entire team is out. The team that's left gets to bat first in the scrimmage or wins a pack of bubble gum or some other prize.

By the end of the season, most players may be prepared to add other elements to the drill. Make each throw bounce once, or have the players throw and catch opposite-handed just for fun.

Workup Game

Contributed by Brig Sorber
Okemos, Michigan

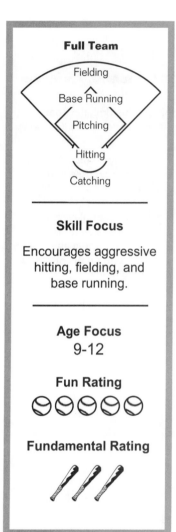

Full Team

Fielding

Base Running

Pitching

Hitting

Catching

Skill Focus

Encourages aggressive hitting, fielding, and base running.

Age Focus
9-12

Fun Rating

Fundamental Rating

This drill is a blast! It's a rotational batting practice with a few twists. When kids are getting a little tired of regular infield and batting practice, this game will really spice things up. It's perfect in situations where kids show up for a game, and the other team forfeits, or the game is cancelled.

☐ The Drill

Put a player in each position (except pitcher), and pitch to the remaining three or four players. If the first batter reaches base, he must score by the time the third batter completes his at-bat. If he scores, he continues to hit. If he doesn't score, he must get his glove and go to right field, the first position in the fielding rotation for this drill. The right fielder then moves to center field. The center fielder takes the position of the left fielder, who moves to the third-base position, and so on. The first baseman comes in to hit. Each hitter must score by the time the second hitter behind him completes his at-bat.

The twist is that any defensive player who makes an out in the air (that is, catches a line drive or a pop-up) gets to cut to the front of the line and go in to bat immediately.

When tentative players realize they can advance to the batter position, they instinctively go after balls more aggressively, taking a risk they normally wouldn't take. Kids must call for all pop-ups and not go too far out of their

Coaching Analysis

After this drill, the coach should analyze the following:

• Did players play the field more aggressively while staying in control?

• Did weaker players take more risks than they normally would have taken — at bat, on the bases, or in the field?

• Did the kids have fun?

immediate positions on fly balls in order to prevent a free-for-all atmosphere. Encourage aggressive play, but not "out of control" play. You may even elect to reward players who simply make great mental plays (for example, getting the lead runner out on a difficult ground ball), or who make an incredible effort or diving play, whether they get the out or not. You can also give an occasional "free pass" to weaker players who make plays that are just a little beyond their expected level of play.

This drill also encourages aggressive base running. If stealing is allowed in your league, it should be allowed in the workup game. The pitcher and catcher should keep runners honest, and attempt to catch them stealing, but most kids will run the bases more aggressively anyway in an attempt to score by the time the second batter behind them completes their at-bats.

As the game progresses, make sure you stop to coach players as necessary. This drill will be tons of fun, and players will tend to get a little bit out of control, but you'll still have opportunities to teach. Try to allow – even encourage – the excess enthusiasm, but take the opportunities you'll have to fix any blatant problems.

Shadow Swinging

Contributed by Daryl Wasano
Oceanside, California

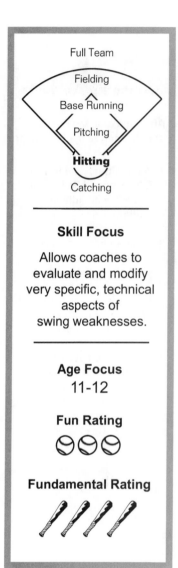

Skill Focus

Allows coaches to evaluate and modify very specific, technical aspects of swing weaknesses.

Age Focus
11-12

Fun Rating

Fundamental Rating

We've rated this drill a "4" for fundamentals because it's simple, but very technically critical to advanced batters. For younger players, a bad swing is generally better than no swing at all, and therefore may not require excessive technical changes. However, at about the age of 11 or 12, the Shadow Swinging Drill may be perfectly appropriate for honing an advanced swing. All it requires is a sunny day.

☐ The Drill

Set up with the sun toward your back so that your shadow is in front of you. Position your first batter next to you and have him assume his normal batting stance. Next, take a baseball and lay it on the ground directly in the head of the player's shadow.

With your eyes fixed on the ball within the shadow, instruct the player to take his full, normal swing. Immediately at the completion of the swing, yell "stop" to the player, at which time he should freeze completely. Is the baseball still in the center of the shadow's head? By staying "quiet", and swinging smoothly without moving their heads, players will be able to hit with control without losing power.

Instruct the player to continue swinging, making note of any movements of the head within the shadow. The ball will not move. Only the shadow will move, depending on the batter's tendencies. If the head of the shadow moves

Coaching Analysis

After this drill, the coach should analyze the following:

- Were hitters able to take full swings while keeping "quiet", with little head motion?

- In cases where hitters had difficulty keeping the ball "in the shadow," were they able to make the necessary mechanical adjustments to "quiet" their head movement?

- After completion of the drill, were the players able to hit live pitches and maintain their "quiet" head movement, particularly at the next practice or game?

to the right (for a right-handed hitter), the batter may be leaning too far toward his back foot through the swing. If

the shadow moves under the ball, the player may be leaning back on his heels, which would cause him to lose power. If the player lunges forward too much with his upper body, swinging primarily with his arms, the head of the shadow will end up to the left of the ball.

Experienced batters have a lot of things going on at one time. They're pulling down, they're turning, they're pivoting their hips, their squishing the bug, they're throwing their hands at the ball, they're rolling their wrists, and so on. In evaluating the mechanics of more experienced batters, each element of the swing can be important. The Shadow Swinging Drill, with the help of a little sunlight, can help you fine-tune the motion of all the combined elements of the swing.

After completing this drill, suggest to the players that they go home and practice their swing in front of the mirror. If they can see the motion visually, they can begin to feel it mentally, ultimately allowing them to fine-tune the motion of their swing.

13 In A Row

Contributed by the Authors

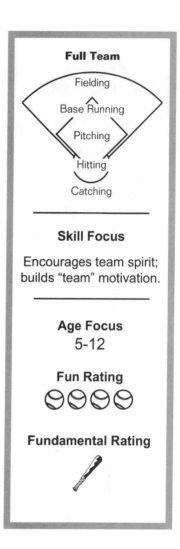

Full Team

Fielding

Base Running

Pitching

Hitting

Catching

Skill Focus

Encourages team spirit; builds "team" motivation.

Age Focus
5-12

Fun Rating

Fundamental Rating

Throughout your coaching career, you will occasionally be challenged to bring your players together as a "team", regardless of the functional successes of the mechanical drills you put those players through. Becoming a unified team may be the most important element of team sports.

With young children, it is imperative that they learn to win or lose gracefully as a team, not just as an individual. One simple, but effective, way to encourage your players to come together as a team is to run 13 In A Row. (If your team has twelve players, then the drill is really "12 In A Row."

☐ **The Drill**

Near the end of a hard practice (particularly the last practice before the first game of the season, and again before the playoffs), line your players up in order, from your weaker defensive players to your stronger ones. Then, one at a time, starting with the "weaker" end, tell players to get into ready position as you throw fly balls to them. The object is for the entire team to get through one round of catches without an error. Seems simple, right?

Now, add a little incentive to the drill. Even include some willing parents. Make a deal with the team. If they make it through the round unscathed, the coaches and parents must run a lap around the field. If any players on the team drop a ball, the players must run a lap, and they must stay

Coaching Analysis

There are no specific skills to analyze for this drill. Instead, success is measured if you see your players coming together as a team, an important part of their overall development.

until they make it through a complete round without an error. For 5-year-olds, the throws might be underhanded from ten feet away. For 12-year-olds, the throws to the more experienced players may be as high as the coach can physically throw the ball. Use your best judgment.

Turn this exercise into a pep rally. Jazz the players up before you start. Explain the drill, then talk it up, including the incentive. Players love to get one up on the parents, so they should be psyched to perform well. Try to make each throw a good match for the player's ability. If the first player drops the ball, you may want to cut the team a break and start over. It's easy to start over right at the beginning, which is why you should start with the weakest fielders, and progress to the strongest ones. By the time the players end the drill in success, they should be totally psyched. Make the most of that excitement and team spirit. Give "high-fives" to each and every player, and encourage them to give "high-fives" to each other. This is all part of the exercise to develop team spirit, which will pay big dividends the next time the team takes the field.

Water-Balloon Hitting

Contributed by Lloyd Rue
Helena, Montana

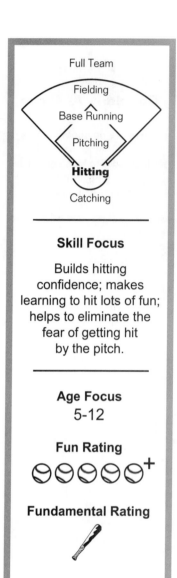

Full Team

Fielding
Base Running
Pitching
Hitting
Catching

Skill Focus

Builds hitting confidence; makes learning to hit lots of fun; helps to eliminate the fear of getting hit by the pitch.

Age Focus
5-12

Fun Rating

Fundamental Rating

Anything you can do to make learning more fun usually makes it more productive, too. Imagine a 96 degree day in July, and twelve kids trying to stay interested in batting practice. Add water balloons, and you'll guarantee instant success and a ton of fun!

☐ The Drill

Buy a few hundred water balloons (the round kind, not the long kind). If there's a water source near the practice field, take a hose and some buckets or trash cans to practice. If there's no water source, fill the balloons to about the size of baseballs, tie them off, put them in the trash cans or buckets, and take them to practice.

After some productive fielding drills, introduce the water-balloon drill. You may even want to use this drill as an incentive for the kids to work hard in the drills leading up to the reward of this drill.

Stand halfway between the pitcher's mound and home plate. Have a player feed you water balloons from the buckets as you pitch them to the remaining players. Pitch one balloon at a time, underhand to each batter. Just instruct the batters to swing away. For the batters who are a little bit nervous about being hit by a pitch, throw a water balloon right at them. They'll love it! The mental imagery is great because when the players hit the water balloons well,

Coaching Analysis

There are no specific skills to analyze for this drill. Instead, the kids should have a blast hitting water balloons!

they explode with great force, the players get wet, and everyone's happy.**

You may choose to turn this drill into a contest by offering a prize to the player who can burst the most water balloons out of, say, ten pitches. The prize can be that the winner gets to hit the coach with a giant water balloon.

For the players who lack confidence while hitting in game situations, shout encouragement like "hit the water balloon." It will put a smile on their faces, and some confidence in their swings.

** Well … not everybody!! Before you run this drill, you should tell parents that kids might get wet. So, when they come to practice that day, parents can plan to send their kids with a bathing suit underneath their practice clothes and a towel. We also suggest that the "home plate" be designated somewhere off the practice diamond so that the real home plate doesn't get all wet and muddy. Finally, after you finish this drill, remind all your players to clean up all the pieces of broken water balloon from around the drill area. THEN everyone will be happy!

Wildcats

Contributed by Phil Swan
Boulder, Colorado

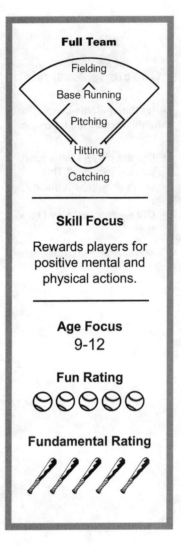

Full Team

Fielding
Base Running
Pitching
Hitting
Catching

Skill Focus

Rewards players for positive mental and physical actions.

Age Focus
9-12

Fun Rating

Fundamental Rating

Wildcats is a game based on points, not runs. Each team scores positive points for things they do well, and negative points for mistakes they make, physically and mentally.

☐ The Drill

Divide the team evenly into three squads of four, keeping in mind the defensive and offensive ability of each player. A coach will pitch the entire game, and eight players (that is, two squads) will be in the field while one squad is at bat. This is a team event, not an individual event. Each squad keeps track of its point total as the game progresses.

Start each batter with a 2-1 count to speed up the game and force more aggressive hitting. Each squad hits until they reach their third out.

Offensive points are scored as follows:

Single = 1 point
Double = 2 points
Triple = 3 points
Home Run = 4 points
Grand Slam = 5 points
Walk = 1 point
Run scored = 2 points
Stolen Base = 1 point
Getting picked off = -3 points

Coaching Analysis

After this drill, the coach should analyze the following:

• Did the players have fun playing wildcats? This game should be a blast!

• Did each squad play like a team?

Double play = -3 points
Striking out looking = -3 points
Reaching base safely = 2 points

Defensive points are scored as follows:

Spectacular play = 5 points
Fly out = 2 points
Ground out = 3 points
Double play = 5 points
Throwing out base stealer = 3 points
Triple play = 10 points
Getting an out in a rundown = 4 points

Bonus points can be scored as follows:

Sacrifice Bunt = 4 points
Successful squeeze play = 5 points
Great attitude or sportsmanship = 5 points
Poor attitude or sportsmanship = -5 points
Anything positive from a weak player = 3 points

These are just suggested point values and can be modified to suit your coaching style. You may also want to recruit one or two parent volunteers to help keep track of points scored during this drill.

As the batting squad finishes, those players move to catcher and outfield positions. Outfielders (and catcher) move to infield positions, and infielders come in to bat.

Mess-Around Game

Contributed by Steve Wagner
DeMotte, Indiana

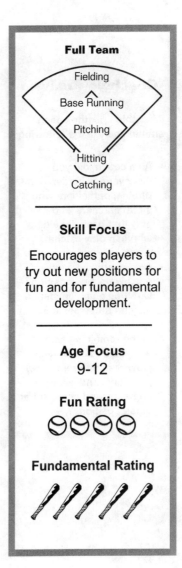

Full Team

Fielding
Base Running
Pitching
Hitting
Catching

Skill Focus

Encourages players to try out new positions for fun and for fundamental development.

Age Focus
9-12

Fun Rating

Fundamental Rating

This is a drill in which you allow kids to play whatever positions they want to try. It's up to them! This game should take place during the second half of the year, with older or more experienced teams, ages nine and up. The kids who wanted to pitch all year will have a chance to pitch. The kid who couldn't wait to wear all that catcher's gear will finally have his chance. Remember that boy who kept begging to try shortstop or first base in the beginning of the season, but didn't have the ability for a key infield position? Now that he's got much of the season under his belt, his improved skills may warrant a shot at a key position in the mess-around game.

☐ The Drill

Start by dividing into two even teams. Have parents and coaches play positions that aren't requested. Next, ask the weaker players which positions they would like to try. If several players want to try the same position, such as pitcher, let them know that you'll be switching every inning or two, so that everyone will get a chance to try several positions.

If you have one or two bashful players who aren't inclined to try new challenges on the baseball field, this would be the time to encourage them to do so, provided that they have the basic skills to play a position safely. You'll be surprised by the amount of "new position" players you'll find during

Coaching Analysis

After this drill, the coach should analyze the following:

• As a coach, did you discover any hidden gems (that is, outfielders who pitch, catchers who can play first base, infielders who can play catcher)?

• As players, did each kid discover a new position? Did they gain confidence playing those positions?

• In the remaining games, will you be able to use players in different (new) positions, and will they be happy and confident at those positions?

this drill. You never know, you may have been sticking the next Nolan Ryan in right field until now.

For the team on offense, allow the weaker players to bat early in the order to boost their confidence and give them more chances to hit. Have one or two coaches or parents help each team while they're batting, giving signals, encouraging bunting or stealing, and keeping players interested and enthusiastic. This isn't the time for specific mechanical instruction to hitters. It's the time for lots of positive encouragement.

As you prepare to start the game, remind defensive players of key fundamentals for each given position. Remind catchers to offer a big target, protect their throwing hand, and to drop down to block wild pitches with the body. Pitchers should be reminded to take their time, stay balanced, and follow through. The most important thing for your first baseman to remember is to move his feet to go after bad throws first, then worry about the base or the runner.

Infielders should remember to field balls like alligators (see "Ready, Alligator, Crowhop" in Coaches' Favorite Drills) and to use the gorilla posture (see "Gorilla Grounders & Gorilla Races" in Coaches' Favorite Drills). Outfielders need to be reminded that their first step should always be backward on fly balls, and throws should be directed to the waving cutoff man. Throughout the game, continue to remind players of specific fundamentals for specific positions.

3
Coaches'
Memorable
Stories

This section contains a collection of personal stories — some humorous, some touching, some inspirational — shared by our hometown hero coaches as we spoke with them.

Use these stories as you wish; browse through them for your personal enjoyment, share them with your fellow coaches, or read them to your team to create that inspirational moment at the end of a practice or just before a game.

These experiences, all of them true, relate the joy and ultimate value of playing and coaching the sport of baseball.

Take Two

Contributed by Jay Hinson
Cheraw, South Carolina

When coaching young players, it's always important to teach them the fundamentals of each field position as well as review with them the basic language of baseball. You've got to make sure that all your players understand the words and phrases that they may hear when they are up at bat or out on the playing field.

I know from experience. One season, I was coaching very young kids in a T-ball league. One of my better hitters came up to bat. He lined his bat up against the tee, took a big swing, and hit the ball pretty hard. He started running as fast as he could towards first base and I was pretty excited, cheering and hollering at him, "Take two! Take two!" All of a sudden I saw him stop in mid stride. He turned around, and with a puzzled look on his face, he yelled back at me, "Take two WHAT, coach?"

What a great coaching moment that was!

Split Decision

Contributed by Russ Thompson
Keene, New Hampshire

I've been coaching for the last nine years now. But, even though I played baseball in high school and in college, I didn't really have any clue how to coach kids.

I'll never forget the very first practice at the start of my youth coaching career. I had volunteered to coach 8- and 9-year-olds. I started the practice by gathering the whole team around home plate. We introduced ourselves, and then I asked the group how many of them had ever played baseball before. Most of them raised their hands or nodded yes. So, I said, "O.K., now we're going to start with some basic fielding skills. Everybody go on down to first base." Then half the team went towards first base while half the team jogged on down to third.

I learned a lot about coaching kids that season!

Endless Runner

Contributed by Ryan Callaham
Round Rock, Texas

Young players with little playing time and experience can get confused about when they should try to run to first base and when they shouldn't when they're up at bat. This happens a lot with foul balls, or when the situation comes up, according to our league rules, where the ball is dropped by the catcher on a third strike and the batter can try to get to first base, basically like a steal.

One year, I had a young player who had only played one other season before that year. He really couldn't hit or field very well at all. Well, during one game early in the season, he got up to the plate to hit the ball. On the first strike, the catcher completely missed the ball and my batter heard it hit the backstop. So, he dropped his bat and ran like crazy towards first base. Of course, everybody else was confused, so they just kind of stood around and looked at him. He got all the way to first base before I could yell to him, "Sorry, but that was the first strike so you have to come back." He didn't seem too upset as he jogged back to home plate.

He picked up his bat and got ready to go again. The second ball came in, he swung at it and missed, and the ball flew right past the catcher. The batter heard it hit the backstop and he did the exact same thing. When I called him back I tried to explain to him about the third strike rule so he wouldn't have to run again.

Well, this poor kid ended up fouling off three times in a row after that and every single time he hit the ball he ran at top

speed straight to first base. By now, he had made five trips to first base. Finally, he connected with a ball, hitting it right in between the shortstop position and third base. He sprinted down to first base and got there on time. But, at this point he was so confused about the rules that he touched the base, turned right around and walked back to home plate! He looked right at me as if to say, "Well, I messed up again, huh, coach."

Heavy Pressure

Contributed by Tom Allen
Northeast, Maryland

You know the pressures that can be put on young players to hit the ball can be enormous. One time, my team had played a game through to the last inning and we were losing seven to two. Well, during our last turn at bat we rallied, making up five runs so that by the time we had two outs, the score was tied up with the other team.

I was coaching at third base and I looked over at our player, a 12-year-old, who was coming up next — one of our best batters of the season — and he was crying. I knew that this kid's stomach was turning circles because he was thinking that the outcome of the whole game depended on him.

So, I called time out and I walked over to him, put my arm around him and I said, "What's wrong, Sam?" And he said, "My stomach is bothering me, coach." So, I looked straight at him and said, "I know what you're going through, but I'm going to tell you right now, I don't care if you strike out, I don't care if you ground out, I don't care if you hit a home run. So, just settle yourself down and just go out there and hit the ball just like you do every other game. I'm only going to be disappointed in you if you don't swing."

So, I went back over to third base and he started drying himself up. The other kids on the team were all cheering him on. The first ball went by him and it was a strike and he didn't swing at it. I just looked at him but I didn't say anything ... I just cheered him on.

He swung at the next strike and he missed. Then the third strike came and he closed his eyes and swung level to hit a beautiful home run. His team came running out of the dugout and surrounded him. They even soaked him down with ice water. And, guess what, his stomach ache was all better!

Advanced Radiology

Contributed by Bill Sandry
Bettendorf, Iowa

Younger kids can be intimidated or distracted by all sorts of things that adults might never think about. Sometimes, even the name of the other team is enough to strike fear into the minds of young players!

I recently had a player on my team, an 11-year-old who had a phenomenal sense of humor. We were in the middle of a game and my players were trying to complete a first to third play where the ball is thrown through the shortstop. Well, this 11-year-old player is playing shortstop. When the ball is thrown to him, he first looks like he's going to let the ball go through, then, instead, he cuts it off and sends it to the catcher to try to get the player going home. Keep in mind that we're playing a team named "Advanced Radiology."

So, none of the guys were getting this play and this time, when they blew it again, I was really getting frustrated as a coach. I called time and walked out there. I wanted to yell at them because I was so frustrated with them. When I got out there I said, trying to control my anger, "Guys, you know, I want to yell at you. I really want to tell you how bad you are. Now, I'm not going to do that. But, come on guys, this isn't rocket science." And at that moment, the 11-year-old looked right up at me and said, "Yeah, we know coach, we're trying … but coach, we ARE playing against Advanced Radiology!"

All I could do was laugh and say, "How did you come up with that one?!"

Golden Moment

Contributed by Gilbert Lopez
Round Rock, Texas

One of the best things in the world for a coach is to get that feeling of accomplishment from developing a player who has no skills at all in the beginning of the season into a player who, at the end of the season, can catch or throw or even make it to first base safely. Coach Gilbert Lopez experienced that golden moment when he got to watch a weak player accomplish something wonderful.

Coach Lopez had a player on his team one season who didn't know anything about the game. He couldn't throw the ball, he didn't know how to run the bases, and he even held his bat upside down the first time it was placed in his hands. During most games, Coach Lopez put this player in the outfield for his own safety since he didn't know how to handle to ball very well.

Well, in one game, Coach Lopez' team was winning by a large margin of runs, and he saw the opportunity to switch some of his weaker players to more key positions on the field. So, he changed the whole infield … he put the inexperienced player up on the pitcher's mound. The game started up again and the pitcher started throwing balls toward the plate. All of a sudden, the batter connected with a pitch and the ball hopped straight towards the pitcher's mound. Coach Lopez watched as the pitcher ran out to meet the ball. He picked it up and threw it straight to first base, where the runner was called out from the first baseman's successful catch.

For both the young player and his coach, it was one of those golden moments … a fantastic experience … a "game ball" rewarding experience … a post-game team trip to the local hamburger place … a great moment in life!

Smiley

Contributed by Ryan Callaham
Round Rock, Texas

Any coach who volunteers to lead baseball teams over a period of several years, will likely end up with a player at one point who has had little or no experience playing baseball, even at the age of 9 or 10. Coach Ryan Callaham remembers one such player.

At the first practice, he came out onto the field without any knowledge of how the game is played. He couldn't hit, field or throw a baseball properly. He even thought that runs were scored just by successfully reaching first base.

Coach Callaham began the task of patiently teaching the fundamentals of baseball to this player. As one might expect, the player learned at a slow and steady pace throughout the season. But his hitting skills were far below the level of the other team members, and he almost always struck out when he came up to bat. The one thing this player had going for him was attitude. He seemed to love playing baseball, and he usually smiled his way through a game or practice.

Well, as the season progressed to the last few games, and a situation arose where "Smiley" came up at bat during a critical moment that would decide the game. Coach Callaham's team had the tying run on third base with two outs as he watched his novice player move up to the plate and flash him a big smile. The coach hoped that now would be the magic moment where a hit would materialize.

The first pitch was thrown — a beautiful pitch that even a T-baller could have hit — but "Smiley" missed it. The second pitch came over the plate … and "Smiley" missed that one too. But as the third pitch came over the plate, "Smiley" swung his bat and hit the ball, not a strong hit, but a hit just the same. Coach Callaham noticed the incredible look of happiness on "Smiley's" face and, right there, the coach knew he had the season made.

So, where did the ball end up? Well, it was hit straight to first base and "Smiley" was out before he got half-way down the line. But, even as he ran to first base and touched the bag with his foot, "Smiley" was grinning from ear to ear and shaking his hands in the air as if he'd just helped win the World Series for his team.

Bending the Rules

Contributed by Monie Duran
San Dimas, California

Sometimes a coach has to use her best judgment in situations where an opportunity exists to enhance a young player's overall sports experience. Such was the case for Coach Monie Duran one season. She was assigned a young boy to her team who was autistic and had tremendous trouble paying attention during practices and games.

At first, Coach Duran was very reluctant to put this particular player in the infield because she was afraid that he would get hurt. But, as the season progressed, and she continued to work with this player, Coach Duran noticed that the youngster could actually focus on his task and could perform quite well in the infield as long as she kept one hand placed lightly on his shoulder.

So, to give her challenged player a chance to enjoy the baseball season, Coach Duran made a decision to bend the rules. Before each game she contacted the coach of the opposing team and asked if she could stand next to this player while he was in position on the field. She explained the situation and promised that she wouldn't interfere with any plays or assist him in any way. She just needed to keep a hand on his shoulder so he could remain focused and his attention wouldn't wander.

Coach Duran gave this player a chance to excel and he became a great player for the team. She hopes to see him back on her team again next year.

A Winning Attitude

Contributed by Daryl Wasano
Oceanside, California

At one point or another, every coach is faced with the tough decision of consistency in attitude versus the desire to win. Such was the case with Coach Wasano in a state tournament game with his 9- to 10-year-old team one season.

Coach Wasano had always told his players that his rule for "no bad attitude" applies in every situation and to every player, even if he had to pull the best player from the field or the batting order, even if it happens at a critical point in a game. During the state tournament, Coach Wasano's team was down four runs to two late in the game, but had runners on first and second base. Coach found himself having to substitute a batter for another player who he had pulled out of the game earlier because he'd thrown a temper tantrum.

Although the substitute was a decent ball player, he was a poor hitter, and he was visibly nervous about stepping up to the plate with the game on the line. So, Coach Wasano called a time out, walked over to the player and encouraged him as much as possible. "Look, just go up there, take a deep breath, and then just put the bat on the ball. I don't care where you hit the ball. Just try to connect with the ball."

The batter stepped up to the plate, gritted his teeth, and swung at the first pitch. The bat struck the ball and it flew out towards second base, where the second baseman made an error and allowed the bases to become loaded. Then, the next batter hit a base clearing double and Coach Wasano's team went on to win the game six runs to four.

Had Coach Wasano brought the player with the bad attitude back into the game to hit during that critical moment, the entire team would have watched their coach's commitment to his own principles fade into the dirt. But, the decision to take a chance and stick to his ideals paid off as a great life lesson for all his team players.

Who's on 2nd?

Contributed by Jon Brainard
San Dimas, California

There was a season when I was coaching 8- and 9-year-olds. It was a very rainy year so we didn't have a lot of practices before our first game. Well, to instill some confidence in the kids in the outfield so they would know what to do when they got the ball, I said, "Just remember, everything goes to second base." I also told my infielders, "Everything goes to second base … throw it to second … throw it to second."

Well, of course, in the first inning of the game, the other team got a player on first base and their next batter hit the ball straight out into right field. The runner on first started going to second just as my right fielder picked up the ball and immediately threw it straight towards second base … great throw. Well, in my eagerness to get throws to second base, I had forgotten to tell any of my infielders that they have to cover second base when the ball is thrown from the outfield. So, they all stood there watching that beautiful throw hit the base and bounce right away! With younger, players you have to remember to cover all the details.

Squish the Bug

Contributed by Lloyd Rue
Helena, Montana

Little kids are so literal in their interpretation of a coach's comments that you've got to be watchful of it. I coached 6- and 7-year-olds one year. I had decided to try teaching baseball to these kids using some of the same basic drills that I use for slightly older players.

So, I began to teach my players all the hitting fundamentals including hand placement, balance, flexed knees, positioning of the head and eye, and so on. When we would work with them on the stride and the turn, I would often tell them to "squish the bug" with their back leg as they turned their hip.

I continued with these detailed drills for about six or eight weeks until I had developed the best hitting team in the league. It really seemed to work well for most kids. But, I had one little player who was probably the least athletic player on the team. He was a wonderful little boy with really great, supportive parents, but he just always struggled to hit the ball.

He just couldn't do it. I tried working with him, trying not to overdo my instruction and break his confidence. But, as much as I gave him personal attention, he just couldn't get the hang of it. On top of everything, he developed this really dramatic front leg kick every time he swung. His knee would come up above his waist and he'd slam it down hard on the ground. I kept telling him not to lift his leg so high, to just stride forward. But, he'd not pay any attention.

Every time he swung the bat, he'd lose his balance and fall over because of this kick.

This went on for at least half of the regular season. Finally, out of my own frustration, I asked him, "What are you doing? Why do you keep kicking your leg out like that?" And he looked up at me with a very serious and sincere look on his face and answered, "But, coach you keep yelling out to squish the bug." I realized that every time he came up to bat, I'd tell him not to lift his leg up, then the next thing I'd yell to him was to squish the bug and that would make him lift his leg up even higher. He was doing EXACTLY what his coach was asking him to do!

Sneaking In

Contributed by JC Petersen
Okemos, Michigan

Sometimes the element of surprise is a worthwhile strategy to use in games, even if it isn't intentional. One season, we won a tournament game in the last half inning all because one of our players lost count of the number of outs on the field. This kid was on third base, waiting for a hit to get him home. Another one of our players had just struck out, making the second out on our team that inning. But, our player on third base had lost count of the number of outs we had and thought that the third out had just been made.

I was coaching third base and I began to focus on our next batter, giving him signs and watching how he set himself up to hit. Everyone else on both teams was also focusing on the next batter. So, while we were all distracted, our "confused" player on third base just casually started walking down the third base line towards home, his head down and his stride lacking any sort of energy … he told us later that he was heading for the dugout to get his gear all packed up.

Suddenly, I notice that this player is walking in and I can't figure out what he is doing. I see the catcher holding the ball behind home plate and looking at our player. Everyone else on the field is just watching him slowly walk down the line towards home. By the time I noticed him, he was too far away for me to call him back to third base, so I hesitated for a moment, then I yelled out, "Mike … uh … touch home." Before the catcher could react, Mike took three steps and touched home plate, scored us a run, and won the game! It was the most casual, nonchalant steal I've ever seen!

Patience Rewarded

Contributed by Tom Sutton
Germantown, Maryland

I've had this one player on my team for several years. Now, this player has real talent. He has a very good arm but he just can't get to the basic principle of throwing so he tends to throw side arm all the time and he throws the ball wild a lot. I've also never been able to teach him the proper mechanics for hitting and other baseball fundamentals. You see, this kid has a lot of learning disabilities, including Attention Deficit Disorder.

He also didn't have a lot of confidence in himself. Over the years, I had watched him several times get up to bat, then just bow out if a hard pitch was thrown. He would develop sudden stomach aches when it came time for him to get up to bat. The team took a lot of outs for him. Even when he did decide to go up to bat, he usually struck out.

Well, during his fourth season with me, we were playing in the championship game and we were up at bat in the top of the fifth inning with a tie score, two outs, and a runner at third. It was this player's turn at bat. He decided to give it a try and, to my amazement, he turned on a pitch from a very good pitcher and lined it into left field for a solid base hit. His hit drove in the base runner and started a four run rally.

His teammates were cheering and I had a tear in my eye because I knew what this hit had meant, not only to us as a team, but to this kid. Then I happened to glance up at his mom and I saw her crying too. She couldn't believe that her son had finally come through this time … in a huge way too.

I can even remember how many times I saw this player so frustrated and how much patience it took to keep working with him and encouraging him. I had figured that there was just no way to get to this kid. I can't explain what happened to him that night when he made that hit, but maybe he just put some things together that he had learned and did it. All I know it that it was such a special moment, and one that we will both always remember… after four years, the big hit in the big game.

Laughing in the Dugout

Contributed by Richard Nagata
Aiea, Hawaii

One thing I tell my team players, an important thing that they need to remember always, is to have the proper attitude and work ethics when they are practicing or playing baseball. Good ethics and attitude will catch the eye of most coaches and will help them to go as far as possible in baseball, whether they eventually play the sport for their high school or continue to play at the recreational level. I also remind them that they have to stay loose and have fun playing the game.

In 2000, I was coaching a team who had made it to the state tournament and the players had all done really well. We ended up winning the tournament that year in large part because all the boys had a really good attitude. Our team had a mix of players — some were real fun loving and some were more serious, but all of them had positive attitudes.

During one game we had a large rain delay, over an hour — you know how it rains all the time in Hawaii. My kids kept themselves real loose, not only physically but also mentally during the entire delay. Some of them had their CD player head gear on and were listening to music and singing and laughing. A coach from the other dugout even began to notice that we were having such a fun time and I think that gave us a psychological advantage.

At one point, when I inquired as to what music they were playing, my kids even challenged me to put the headphone on. As soon as I did, they blasted the music and my ear

drums! The whole team was laughing at their coach who couldn't take the loud sounds very well.

When it was time to return to the game, these kids knew how to do their job and they got right down to business. We came back after the rain delay and won the game.

A Royal Pain

Contributed by Brig Sorber
Okemos, Michigan

One year, I had this kid on my team who was just your typical royal pain. He wouldn't listen to anything I asked him to do, he didn't pay attention during the game, and so on. I had known about this player from previous seasons and, in fact, I wouldn't have even accepted this kid onto my team except that his mom practically begged me to take him.

So, I took him and, as I expected, he was just a real royal pain. He wouldn't listen and finally I started just sticking him out in left field all the time. Well, at one game during the season, our team was in the field and I saw the batter for the other team just hit a rope out towards left field. I mean, this was a hard hit. As I watched the ball flying through the air, I saw my left field player, the "royal pain," stick his glove up into the air. Now, keep in mind that I could have thrown a hundred balls to this player and he wouldn't have caught even a single one. But, this was his moment and he caught that ball perfectly to make the third out for that inning.

Well, the whole team ran out to the field and we met him at third base. I had him in my arms and I was jumping up and down. We didn't even end up wining that game, but next morning his mom called me and said, "You can't believe what that catch has done for this kid. His whole attitude has changed." You know, you just can't coach that stuff … that's just the magic of baseball.

Chemistry Counts

Contributed by Colonel John Parker
Hilton Head Island, South Carolina

Never discount the power of team chemistry in selecting players for All Star teams. In the selection of the All Star team coming out of Hilton Head recently, we coaches had selected 12 of the 13 players for our 9- and 10-year-old team. All of the players we had selected were 10 years old ... you know, the biggest and the strongest as well as the players with the most experience.

For the last player selection, we decided on a 9-year-old player who was very, very fast, but who had only hit one foul ball during the entire regular season — he'd only put his bat on the ball one time. But, we coaches all knew that he was very fast and we thought that we'd work on his bunting and might use him as a pinch runner as well.

Well, this All Star team did very well and ended up playing in the state championship game. We were ahead by only one to zero in the top of the sixth inning in this game when the 9-year-old came up to bat. Up to this point, he hadn't even gotten a single hit during the playoff series, all the way through the sub-districts and into this game.

Well, this player laid down a perfect bunt to become a base runner and then later on ended up scoring the "insurance run" to win the game.

The interesting thing, and even more important than the bunt itself, was that this player made the team primarily because of his great attitude and his chemistry with the other players. This was a kid who was smaller and younger than a lot of the kids we could have selected, but he had a big heart and all he wanted to do was give 110% all the time. He accepted whatever role the coaches felt was most appropriate for him. This player became a "cheerleader" for the team and supported all the other players. At nine years of age, he understood the importance of playing that role for his team.

By the way, this All Star team made it all the way to win the state championship and then on to become overall champions in the Dixie Youth League World Series.

Winning the Race

Contributed by Tom Allen
Northeast, Maryland

We all know that people are motivated by all sorts of different things in life. Companies often use rewards to motivate their employees, teachers use rewards to motivate their students, doctors use rewards to motivate their patients. It's no different with youth baseball players. A coach can observe his or her players and figure out what motivates each one. Then, when necessary, the coach can figure out ways to work those individual motivations into games.

Such was the case with Coach Tom Allen. Coach Allen remembers a player on one of his teams who was an excellent pitcher, but he tended to get very anxious during tight games and he would stop concentrating on his pitching technique. This particular player also loved NASCAR racing. He was always talking about his favorite driver, Sterling Marlin, and going to watch a race at the Dover Race Track in Dover, Delaware.

In one game during the season, Coach Allen's team was playing a very tough opposing team. The good pitcher was put in for the first four innings to face this team. As he pitched through the first inning, Coach Allen could sense the anxiety building up in his pitcher. By the middle of the second inning, the opposing team was loading up the bases and scoring runs on walks.

So, Coach Allen called a timeout and walked out to the pitcher's mound. To get his pitcher's mind off the game,

Tom started talking about NASCAR. "Did you know that I'm actually going to Dover tomorrow?" the coach said. "And I tell you what, I'll try my hardest to get you Sterling Marlin's autograph when I go. That's a promise. It doesn't matter to me if you throw a ball or a strike on the next pitch. It doesn't matter if our team wins or loses the game today. I'll still try my hardest to get you that autograph."

A big smile came over the pitcher's face and Coach Allen could see the anxiety leaving his mind. When the game started up again, the pitcher struck out the next three batters. As it turned out, the game was just about a no-hitter after that.

The next day Coach Allen did go to Dover and waited over two hours to get an autograph of Sterling Marlin for his player. Both Coach Allen and his pitcher had "won their race."

Teaming with Spirit

Contributed by the Authors

Sometimes a team becomes so responsive to positive coaching and becomes so cohesive during the season that they begin to motivate themselves. Such was the case one season with Coach Rod Hudson's kid-pitch level team, the fabulous "A"s.

Coach Hudson had a feeling about this team from the time they met for the first practice. If he looked around at his players, he couldn't really name anybody a star. However, whenever they practiced and played together, they seemed to get the job done. Everybody seemed filled with a contagious positive attitude, so Coach Hudson decided to build on their natural energy, speaking to them at every practice about supporting each other, showing leadership, and cheering each other on whenever they were together on the ball field.

The season began very well. However, when the "A"s finished the first half of the season at six wins and zero losses, Coach Hudson became a little concerned that they would become so used to all their success that it might prevent them from keeping their positive spirit at every game. So, he sat them all down and told them, "You guys have all done an outstanding job so far this season and I'm really proud of the leadership and team spirit I see out there on the ball field. Your positive attitude has, in large part, been the reason you've gone 6 and 0. But, at some point, you know, the team is going to lose a game, and I don't want you to be too disappointed."

As he finished speaking, he noticed that the players were all looking around at each other, some with confused expressions on their faces. Finally, one player spoke up and said, "But, coach, we're not going to lose. We're all winners, right?"

Well, of course, Coach Hudson had let them know on numerous occasions that they were all "winners", but he had also emphasized to them that they could each be winners with attitude and leadership, not necessarily scores in a game. However, the players insisted that they were a winning team … no matter what … so Coach Hudson decided to leave them to their dreams. "All I can do," he figured, "is support them and keep encouraging their natural team spirit."

As the season progressed, the "A"s continued to win their games and display the positive energy that Coach Hudson had modeled for them … they cheered for each other and congratulated each other on good plays, they even consoled each other when one of them struck out at bat.

What became of Coach Hudson's worries about the team's disappointment at their first loss? Well, he never got the chance to find out how they would react… the team finished the season at 16 wins – 0 losses, powered on natural team spirit and positive coaching!

Pee Wee Pete

Contributed by Jeff Mathis
DeMotte, Indiana

For some kids, it's a scary thing to step up to the plate to bat. Even if they are hitting off a tee or even if everybody else is also struggling to hit, some kids just feel like the entire world is watching and waiting for them to miss the ball.

Coach Jeff Mathis remembers a young player who just froze every time he'd get up to bat. Pee Wee Pete was a little guy. It seemed like he was barely taller than the bat he was trying to hold. Inevitably, whenever Coach Mathis would send this player seven soft underhand pitches (the rule for coach-pitch level in his league), this player wouldn't swing at any of them.

During practices, Coach Mathis patiently worked and worked and worked with this player. Finally, most the way through the season, Pee Wee Pete was starting to swing at the ball. He even made a few hits at practice, but never during the game ... until Coach Mathis came up with a brilliant idea.

At that evening's practice, when Pee Wee Pete came up to bat, Jeff momentarily turned his back to home plate, grabbed a ball, and used a knife to unravel a couple of the stitches in the ball's leather skin. Then he turned back to Pete and told him to swing at the next pitch. Pee Wee connected with the ball and it rolled out toward the pitcher's mound. Coach Mathis ran over to grab it, and exclaimed, "Wow! Look at that Pete! You almost knocked the leather off that ball!" He showed it to the young player.

Then, as Coach Mathis walked back to the pitcher's mound, he knocked a couple more stitches out of the ball. Then he threw another pitch ... and when Pete hit it there was more ball coming out of the leather.

At the next league game, Coach Mathis used the same ball when Pete came up to bat. The coach pitched it to Pete, he swung, and he hit the ball towards first base. As the ball rolled down the baseline, the leather came all the way off the ball. The crowd began to cheer as Coach Mathis ran over to Pete, hoisted him to his shoulders, and ran with him all the way around the bases. Pete's mom was crying and his dad was grinning ear-to-ear.

Coach Mathis sees Pete's friends once in a while....he's much older now... and they say he still has the ball leather up on his shelf in his bedroom.

Whiffle® Ball at Midnight

Contributed by Phil Swan
Boulder, Colorado

No matter how you look at things, it's always tough to lose a championship, especially when your team is playing in the final game at the state level. That happened to Coach Swan's team. They lost the state championship after being state champs for the previous two years. Worse yet, the team that beat them had lost to Coach Swan's team twice earlier in the season.

As one can imagine, Coach Swan's players were pretty devastated for the first hour or so after the game was finished. They had sacrificed a tremendous amount and worked very hard to get to that level. They were a great team — half as big as many of their opposing teams, but almost always twice as fast when it came to making plays and running the bases.

The amazing thing is that, by the time the team got to the banquet room they had reserved at a local restaurant for their team party, the kids were already starting to recover emotionally. They were laughing and joking and acting like normal. In fact, it was that night at the traditional end-of-the-season sleepover at Coach Swan's house, where the true team spirit emerged once again. Around midnight, Coach Swan (who had apparently escaped the sleepover party room to catch a few winks himself) got a phone call from his neighbor. "Did you know," she said, "that the kids are all out in your backyard right now?"

Coach Swan sprang out of bed and headed to his backyard to assess the situation. When he got there, he found his entire team outside playing backyard baseball with a Whiffle® Ball at midnight! They had all long since forgotten about the championship loss.

It was at that moment that Coach Swan looked around at his team and realized that, for these kids, playing baseball was mostly about good friendships and memories … not about wins and losses. These kids knew they had given it their best, but they also knew that life goes on after baseball.

Index

Quick Order Form

Fax Orders: Complete this form and fax it to 301-527-0771.
Telephone Orders: Call toll free 1-800-527-6991. Have your credit card ready.
Secure Website Orders: www.crmpublishers.com

Postal Orders: CRM Publishers
PO Box 5706
Derwood, Maryland 20855-0706. USA.

Please send me the following book order:

Product	# Copies	Price Total
Collective Coaching Wisdom for Youth Baseball For 1-11 books, multiply # copies desired by $19.95. For 12-24 copies, multiply # copies desired by $16.95. Please call 800-527-6991 for orders of more than 24 books or orders shipping outside the U.S.		
(For orders shipping to Maryland addresses, add 5% sales tax) **Tax**		
Shipping		
Total		

Shipping Charges*
*Use this rate chart to determine your shipping charges. We ship single books to U.S. destinations via USPS Priority Mail and two or more books via FedEx Ground. Please call for orders shipping outside the U.S.

No. of books	Shipping, Packing, & Handling	No. of books	Shipping, Packing, & Handling	No. of books	Shipping, Packing, & Handling	No. of books	Shipping, Packing, & Handling
1	$4.00	7	$10.75	13	$15.25	19	$19.75
2	$7.00	8	$11.50	14	$16.00	20	$20.50
3	$7.75	9	$12.25	15	$16.75	21	$21.25
4	$8.50	10	$13.00	16	$17.50	22	$22.00
5	$9.25	11	$13.75	17	$18.25	23	$22.75
6	$10.00	12	$14.50	18	$19.00	24	$23.50

Payment:

Check or money order (no COD's) payable to: CRM Publishers, or charge: (CIRCLE ONE)

AMEX   VISA   MasterCard   NOVUS

Card number:

Name on card: (please print)

Expiration Date:

Signature:

Ship to this address:

Name: _____

Address: _____

_____

City: _____ State: _____ Zip: _____

Daytime Phone: (_____) _____
AREA CODE

Email: _____

League Fundraising Book Bundle

Get FREE *books* for your coaches and players!

Here's how it works ...

1. Purchase the fundraising bundle that includes:
    -   12 copies of "Collective Coaching Wisdom for Youth Baseball" at 15% off list price
    -   150 copies of Kids' Baseball Fun & Activity Book at 40% off list price

2. As a league fundraiser, sell all the Kid's Fun & Activity Books for $5.00 to $10.00 each to registered players.

3. Your sales revenue entirely covers the cost of both kids' and coaches' books plus profit left over!

Kids' book includes:

*   word searches
*   dot-to-dots
*   mazes
*   crossword puzzles
*   trivia
*   word games
*   situation plays
*   design a ball park
*   daily practice skills

... and more!

More Information:

CRM Publishers
800-527-6991
www.crmpublishers.com